William Robert Wilde, Royal Irish Academy Museum

A Descriptive Catalogue of the Antiquities in the Museum of

the Royal Irish Academy

William Robert Wilde, Royal Irish Academy Museum

A Descriptive Catalogue of the Antiquities in the Museum of the Royal Irish Academy

ISBN/EAN: 9783744727549

Printed in Europe, USA, Canada, Australia, Japan

Cover: Foto ©ninafisch / pixelio.de

More available books at **www.hansebooks.com**

A DESCRIPTIVE CATALOGUE

OF

THE ANTIQUITIES

OF

GOLD

IN THE

Museum of the Royal Irish Academy.

BY

W. R. WILDE,

VICE-PRESIDENT OF THE ROYAL IRISH ACADEMY.

Illustrated with Ninety Wood Engravings.

DUBLIN:
HODGES, SMITH, AND CO., GRAFTON-STREET.
LONDON: WILLIAMS & NORGATE, HENRIETTA-STREET, COVENT GARDEN.
1862.

DUBLIN:
Printed at the University Press,
BY M. H. GILL.

TABLE OF CONTENTS.

	Page.
GOLD, Introduction to,	1
Analysis of Gold,	7
The Irish Crown,	8
Lunulæ,	10
Minds,	12
Diadems,	19
Gorgets,	30
The great Clare Find,	31
Necklaces,	31
Beads,	36
Ear-rings,	37
Fillets and Hair-Bands,	38
Breast-pins and Brooches,	40
Annular Bracelets and Armillæ,	45
Unclosed Rings and Armillæ,	49
Ingots,	50
Armillæ,	51
Mammillary Fibulæ,	57
Flat-plated Fibulæ,	63
Torques,	70
Waist-Torques,	72
Neck-Torques,	73
Finger-Rings,	81
Circular Plates,	82
Bracteate Medals,	83
Boxes,	84
Bullæ,	85
Miscellaneous Articles,	87, 89
Ring-Money,	88

CATALOGUE

OF

THE MUSEUM OF ANTIQUITIES

OF THE

ROYAL IRISH ACADEMY.

CLASS V.—METALLIC MATERIALS.

ORDER V.—GOLD.

INTRODUCTION.

ALL probability gold—in Irish, *Or*—was, for the reasons stated at page 354 of Vol. I., the metal with which the primitive inhabitants of Ireland were first acquainted. A greater number and variety of antique articles of gold have been found in this than in any other country in North-Western Europe, from the Alps to the utmost inhabited limits of Norway, or Sweden. Records of these discoveries can be traced through all the works relating to the archæology and history of Ireland, published during the last two hundred years, and are also preserved in the unpublished Minutes, as well as the printed Proceedings and Transactions of the Academy. These antique manufactured specimens of gold for the most part consist of articles connected with personal decoration, such as ornaments worn on the head,—diadems, tiaras, lunulæ, hair-plates, and ear-rings; those used for the neck, as, for example, gorgets, small torques, flattened beads, globular balls, and necklaces; for the breast, as circular plates, fibulæ, and brooches; for the limbs, as armillæ, bracelets, and finger-rings; and for the chest and waist, in the form of large torques: besides various minor trinkets and miscellaneous articles, such as bullæ; small, circular boxes; penannular-shaped articles, supposed to represent money; bracteate medals, and some other objects of undetermined use. Of all these there are good representations in the magnificent Collection of the Academy, which at present (Jan., 1862) contains as many as three hundred specimens of antique manufactured gold. These, however, are but a small portion of the gold antiquities found in Ireland, even within the past century, the great bulk of which had been melted down by jewellers, long before the institution of the Academy's Museum, about thirty-three years ago. And even during this latter period, far more articles of Irish gold have in all probability found their way to the crucible than have been anywhere preserved as objects of antiquarian or historic interest. Besides those in the Academy, there are many noble specimens of Irish art in the Museum of Trinity College, and in the collections of private individuals, not only in Ireland, but also in England and Scotland; and the majority of the gold articles illustrative of the antiquities of the British Isles, now preserved in the British Museum, are Irish. The ignorance of the finders, the fear of detection, the low antiquarian value heretofore attached to such articles, the want of a law of treasure-trove,*—such as exists in other countries,—the smallness of the fund placed at the disposal of the Academy for the purchase of such articles, rendering it unable to purchase many valuable specimens that have been offered for sale, and

* The Treasury Minute respecting "*Treasure-trove*" in Ireland only came into operation in April, 1861, and its effects have as yet been tested but to a very limited extent.

the apathy and indifference with respect to the preservation of our national antiquities which have prevailed up to a very recent period, have all tended to promote this lamentable dispersion, or destruction, of the golden treasures found beneath the surface of the soil in Ireland during more than a century and a half. How much may have been discovered prior to the commencement of that period, it is now impossible to calculate.

Unlike the weapons and implements of stone, bronze, and iron, discovered in such quantities on ancient battle-fields, or in the beds of rivers, where probably the ford was the scene of hostile strife, gold antiquities are scarcely ever found in drainage operations; neither have they been discovered in any of our Crannoges, or lacustrine habitations, the antiquities of which chiefly consist of implements employed in culinary, household, and domestic use, or personal decorations of bone, bronze, and iron. Gold articles have, for the most part, been found deep below the surface of our bogs, a portion of the peat of which had probably grown over them, where they were dropped in flight, and remained unseen to human eye, until disinterred, centuries after, by the turf-cutter; or hidden, often in quantity, in the earth in upland districts, in the vicinity of the fort or cromlech, or in the neighbourhood of the battle-field. So far as the records of such discoveries are available, it would appear that the south-western moiety of the island has yielded a greater amount of gold than the north-eastern. As yet we have but very slight authentic evidence of gold having been discovered with the remains of the dead, as so frequently occurs in other countries; and therefore we are unable to associate the knowledge of this metal, or the use of any particular style of ornament appertaining thereto, with cremation, or urn-burial, or any of the circumstances under which the relics of either the Pagan or the Christian dead of Ireland have been found. Scattered broad-cast over the country, yet abounding in particular districts, it would (without any exact knowledge being attainable upon the subject) appear that these articles were dropped, or hidden in haste or fear, and possibly at a time when the foe or the invader pressed hotly upon the heels of the fugitive. The present goldsmiths and jewellers of Ireland bear testimony to the fact of the great quantities of antique articles of gold which have been consigned to the crucible,—some estimate that they have purchased as much as £10,000 worth.*

By such assays as have, from time to time, been made of antique manufactured gold found in Ireland, we learn that it is slightly below the present standard of that metal in Great Britain and Portugal, and varies from 18 to 21 carats fine; and, therefore, its intrinsic value is a few shillings less per ounce than that of the mint or sovereign gold. In some of the very fine thin plates or lunulæ, it is found to be as high as $21\frac{1}{2}$ carats, but in no instance is it perfectly pure. The alloy is generally silver and a little copper, but of this the assaymaster takes no special note. In the native ores of Wicklow gold is always found mixed with silver and a little copper; and according to the analysis mentioned by Mr. Calvert, in his "Gold Rocks of Great Britain and Ireland," published in 1853, their proportions were as follows:—gold, 92 oz. 32 dwts.; silver, 6 oz. 17 dwts. 6 grs. Mr. Weaver's assay gave $22\frac{5}{8}$, and that of Mr. Alchorn $21\frac{6}{8}$ carats of pure gold.† By an assay of Wicklow gold,‡ recently made for the author by Mr.

---

* Many of the circumstances relating to gold "finds" were brought under the notice of the Academy by the Author, on the 14th of January, 1861.

† Weaver's Geological Relations of the East of Ireland, Trans. Geol. Soc., London, First Series, vol. v., p. 117, *et seq.*

‡ Besides the Wicklow gold-field, there are other auriferous districts in Ireland; for instance, the counties of Antrim, Tyrone, Derry, Dublin, Wexford, and Kildare. See the detailed account thereof in Mr. Calvert's "Gold Rocks," referred to above. There are several places in Ireland into the names of which the Irish word *Or*, gold, enters; but they do not so much indicate places in which gold was found, as localities associated with other circumstances connected with that metal. Thus, *Gort-an-oir*, 'the field of gold," near Deargrath, in Mugh Femin, derived its name from the circumstance of King Lughaidh Maccon being slain there, whilst he was bestowing gold

Twycross, the Dublin assay-master, it was 1 car. 1½ grs. better than standard, or 23 carats fine, the amount of silver being in the ratio of 6½ dwts. in a pound Troy. A chemical quantitative analysis of another sample, made by Mr. Scott, Secretary to the Geological Society of Dublin, was as follows:—gold, 89 ; silver, 8·1 ; iron, 2·1 ; and a trace of copper. From all these examinations, it would appear that the native gold of this island is either up to or above standard.

These assays and analyses of ores do not, however, present greater variety as to the amount of pure gold than is found in the antique manufactured state; but it must be remembered, that the metal of these articles may have been used for other purposes previously, and so acquired some portions of these alloys. The ring, No. 248, in Case E, is a good example of the colour of the fine native gold of Croghan, in Wicklow. The average price given for our antique golden articles by jewellers and goldsmiths for smelting purposes varies from 65 to 70 shillings per ounce. The antiquarian value is usually £4 per ounce ; but this sum is occasionally increased, according to the rarity of the article, its amount of ornament, its state of preservation, or the peculiar circumstances under which it has been found.* By quantitative analyses made by

---

and silver on the learned men of Erinn, A. D. 225. See Annals of the Four Masters, O'Donovan's translation. The place is now called Derrygrath, near Caher, county of Tipperary. So also *Dun-an-oir*, " the fort of the gold," in Kerry, and another of the same name in the Co. Cork, so called from the fact of hoards of gold having been found there. Other localities are styled *golden*, from the yellow colour of the clay, or from the richness of the soil, or fertility of the district.

* Under the present *Treasure-trove* regulations, the finder of an article has only to bring it to the nearest police officer, from whom he will receive a receipt, by which the Government undertakes to return the article, if not required; or to give, if retained, the "*full value*" thereof; not merely its intrinsic or bullion value, if of metal, but its full antiquarian worth, as determined by the Committee of Antiquities of the Royal Irish Academy, to which body all such articles are submitted for award by the Lord Lieutenant.

The country is deeply indebted to Lord Talbot de Malahide for his valuable influence and assistance in procuring the Treasury Minute, from which it is to be hoped

Mr. J. W. Mallet, and already referred to at page 359 of Vol. I., the following were the proportions in eight specimens :—the quantity of gold varied from 71·48 per cent. in a fragment of a thin neck-torque, No. 200, to 96·90, in a portion of a bracelet, formed of twisted wires, No, 188, both in Case E; and the amount of silver, from 23·67 in the former, to 2·49 in the latter. In the eight examples examined, the proportion of copper varied from 4·62 to 0·12 per cent. The admixture of alloy by our early gold-workers, if such took place, beyond that found in its natural state, or acquired by frequent working, shows an extraordinary amount of metallurgic knowledge, and points to a high state of civilization in the artists by whom it was employed.* An assay which we recently procured of a portion of a large thin lunula, No. 8, in Case A, showed it to be only 1 carat 0¾ grs. less than standard. It would be a matter of interest to discover whether the amount and quality of the alloy was fixed for any particular variety of ornament; but as a yet sufficiently extensive series of assays and analyses have not been made to determine this point.†

In the ancient annals and histories of Ireland, relating to the most remote historic periods, down to the fifteenth cen-

so much benefit will in future be derived, and the intent of which will, we sincerely hope, be made as public as possible by the nobility, clergy, and gentry, and all persons interested in rescuing from the smelting-pot, and preserving in our great National Collection, some of the best materials for our ancient domestic history.

* Gold is red or yellow, according to the amount of copper or silver with which it may be alloyed. From the circumstance of "*red gold*" being frequently specified in our ancient MSS., it would seem to have had a special value attached to it; but whether this red ore was obtained from any particular locality, or was produced by the artificial admixture of a reddening material, is unknown at present.

† In early times the men of Leinster were called "Lagenians of the Gold," from the circumstance of the quantity of gold found in the Co. Wicklow, as already stated at p. 354 of Vol. I.; and besides the entries and references there given, the following extract from the *Book of Leinster* (MS., T. C. D., fol. 246 *a*), for which the author is indebted to the Rev. Dr. Todd, still further explains the appellation :—

"The reason why the men of Leinster are called 'Lagenians of the Gold' is this—

tury, we find more numerous references to gold than in the records of any other country in North-Western Europe. These show that gold, both in the crude and manufactured state, was in frequent use in this country in ancient times. We read of gold in bulk, or by weight, having been paid for ransom (in some instances as much as 300 ounces),* exacted as tribute, given in barter, or for charity. Of wrought gold we have notices of torques and bracelets being worn by distinguished persons; or, in the form of rings and armillæ, being presented as the reward of merit to poets and historians. Instances of all these are numerous; but, as regards the most remarkable and pe-

because in their country gold mines were first discovered in Erin. In the forest south of the Liffey the gold was first smelted, as the poet says—

'Ucadon, the artist of Cualann,
Was the first to inhabit Dord, I assert.
It was in his inviolate, delightful place
That gold was first *boiled* in Erinn;
Upon his woody, sportful lawn,
Long, capacious bellows were blown
By the man of unebbing fame,
In the forests south of the Liffey.'"

That is, the plain of the Liffey, the present Wicklow gold district, from which the river takes its name.

* A. D. 989. When O'Melaughlin gained the battle of Dublin over the Danes, and besieged them in their citadel, now Dublin Castle, they at length yielded to his demand, and gave "*an ounce of gold* for every garden, to be paid on Christmas-night for ever."

A. D. 1029. Amlaff, the Dane, when captured by Mahon O'Reagain, Lord of Bregia, paid as his ransom "twelve hundred cows, sevenscore British horses, and *threescore ounces of gold,* and the sword of Carlus."

A. D. 1151. Turlough O'Brien took with him to Connaught, besides other articles, "*ten ounces of gold.*"

A. D. 1162. When peace was concluded between the Danes and Irish, *one hundred and twenty ounces* of gold "were given by the foreigner to O'Lochlainn, King of Meath;" and "fivescore ounces of gold" were paid by Diarmid O'Melaughlynn to Rory O'Conor, for Westmeath.

A. D. 1168. Dermot Mac Murrough gave *one hundred ounces* of gold to Tiernan O'Rourke for his Einach, or atonement.

A. D. 1169. Donough O'Carroll, Lord of Airghialla, died, "after bestowing *three hundred ounces* of gold, for the love of God, upon clerics and churches."— Annals of the Four Masters, O'Donovan's translation. Dublin: Hodges and Smith.

culiarly Irish, as well as the most valuable specimens, both intrinsically and artistically, which have been discovered, there is no mention in our accessible Annals. They, probably, belong to pre-historic times, and were lost long before the age of writing in this country. Among the most remarkable of these are the beautful diadems, coronets, and other head ornaments in the Academy's Collection.

Had the Irish monarchs or provincial kings crowns? is a question frequently asked. If they had, history is silent on the subject, and we have no records of such being used at the inauguration of kings or chieftains. There is not in Irish history an account of the ceremony of a *coronation*. Two golden articles, however, like caps or helmets, and which may have served as crowns, were found in Ireland during the past century. One of these, figured by Dermot O'Connor, in the introduction to his translation of Keating's "History of Ireland," published in 1723, and of which the accompanying illustration is a *fac-simile*, was discovered in a bog at the Devil's Bit, in the Co. Tipperary, in 1692, and remained for some time in the possession of the Comerford family, by whom it was carried to France, but whether still in existence or not is unknown.

Fig. 537.

It weighed only 5 oz., and must, therefore, have been very thin and slight. Its ornamentation is undoubtedly Irish, and is identical with that on some of our very early golden articles, especially lunulæ and fibulæ, and consists of embossed circles and straight lines, some parallel, and others arranged in angles of the chevron pattern, like those seen in some of the terra-cotta urns of Pagan times.* "Another crown of gold, similar to this,"

---

* The dimensions of that article are not given, and its weight, about 5 oz., shows that it must have been very thin. In the Copenhagen Museum may be seen some says Vallancey, writing in 1783, "was found some years ago on the estate of Mr. Stafford."—See *Collectanea*, Vol. IV., p. 39. *Aisin* is the name used by some comparatively modern Irish writers for a crown or diadem; but it is also applied to a reliquary, and is not a term of much antiquity. At what period the crown known to moderns, and consisting of a coronet more or less raised, and decorated with semicircular bands or hoops passing from one side to the other, was first introduced, has not been clearly stated by writers, although, from the shape, it would appear to have had its origin in the mural crown of classic nations. The earliest insignia of power, rank, or sovereignty, would appear to have been a bands or fillets, as shown on some of the most ancient coins and gems. The fact that for centuries prior to the Anglo-Norman invasion there was not any *sole* monarch of Ireland, may account for the circumstance of there being no such national regalia; while those magnificent golden diadems still preserved in the Academy's Collection, and which, probably, belonged to kings and queens in the days of the Irish pentarchy, far surpass any ornaments of the kind of a similar age discovered in North-Western Europe.*

thin golden cup-shaped vessels, highly ornamented in the Scandinavian style of art which were found suspended in ancient tombs. See, in particular, Plate 61, Fig. 280, in Worsaae's *Nordiske Oldsager*, 1859. If we reverse the drawing of the so-called Irish crown given above, and place it beside one of these northern vessels, the resemblance is very striking; or, if we reverse the latter, it quite as much resembles a cap, or crown, as that given in the foregoing illustration. Banquetting vessels of the precious metals were not unknown to the early Irish. See, among other notices, the Fragments of Irish Annals, copied by Dubhaltach Mac Firbisigh, and published by the Archæological and Celtic Society, with a translation and notes by the late Dr. O'Donovan, in 1860.

* *Irish Crowns.*—I am aware that the opinion expressed in the text respecting the Irish crown, at least as we now understand the term, is contrary to that asserted by O'Flaherty, in the Ogygia, and Lynch, in his Cambrensis Eversus, as well as by Ward, M'Curtin, and other writers; but as yet I have not met with any authority which describes such an article, or relates the circumstances and ceremonial of a coronation. In Scandinavia, which, next to our own country, is rich in antique gold de-

All the golden articles are arranged in six upright cases, placed in strong fire-proof safes, on the ground-floor at the eastern and western ends of the Museum.

SPECIES V.—PERSONAL DECORATIONS.

LUNULÆ, or LUNETTES.—In Irish, *Mind* or *Minn.*—The most frequently discovered gold ornament—and that in which the type, both in shape, size, and style of decoration, is most decidedly fixed—is a thin crescentic, or moon-shaped plate, with the extremities formed into small, flat, circular discs, at right angles with the plane of the article, and which is now known by the name of *lunula*,* or lunette, of which the following illustrations are good examples. This engraving, from No. 2, in Case **A**, represents one of the largest and most perfect of these ornaments. It is 9 inches across from out to out, $5\frac{7}{8}$ in the clear of the hollowed part, which is not a perfect circle; and measures $2\frac{1}{8}$ deep in the widest portion at top.

The ornamentation, which is very minute and elaborate, was in this, and in almost all similar specimens, evidently effected by a series of fine chisel-edge punches, the indentations made by which can in some instances be observed on the plain reverse side. The lines which surround the edges would, however, appear to have been produced by the graver. It is formed

---

corations, no such regalia have been discovered; but bronze circlets, diadems, and hair ornaments, for a like purpose, abound. For some account of the inauguration of the Irish Christian kings and chieftains, see O'Donovan's translation of "The Genealogies, Tribes, and Customs of Hy-Fiachrach," printed by the Irish Archæological Society, 1844, p. 425. Even when Conaire the Great was invested with the sovereignty of Ireland, at Tara, and stood upon the *Lia Fail*, which, it is said, roared under him in acknowledgment of his right, we do not read of a crown being placed on his head. The ancient romance of the *Táin Bó Cuailgne* mentions that Meadhbh, Queen of Connaught, went to battle in a chariot, with a *minn* or diadem on her head, but we are not given any description of the article.

* We find the the term "*Lunula*" first applied to these articles by the learned Pococke, then Bishop of Meath, in his article on the subject of Irish gold antiquities found in 1742, and printed in the Archæologia, vol. ii., p. 37.

CLASS V.—METALLIC MATERIALS: GOLD—LUNULÆ.   11

of a plate of very pure gold of paper thinness, and weighs 3 oz. 4 dwts. 3 grs. This is one of the few remaining speci-

Fig. 538. No. 2.

mens of the Academy's original Collection, and is believed to be that found near Killarney, and *presented by Lord Kenmare in* 1778, as described in the MS. Minute-Book of the Committee of Antiquities, vol. i., p. 50.

The Academy's Collection of lunulæ at present consists of fifteen specimens, eleven of which are complete, although a few are in fragments. They are all arranged in Case **A**, at the eastern end of the ground-floor, and vary from $5\frac{3}{4}$ to $11\frac{1}{8}$ inches wide.

In the absence of any distinct reference in Irish history to these crescentic or moon-shaped ornaments, the mode in which they were worn is still a subject of discussion amongst antiquaries,—some asserting that they were hung round the neck like gorgets; while others, with more apparent reason, believe that they were placed upright on the head, with the flat, terminal plates applied behind the ears. In this latter position they would be much more ostensible and attractive than if suspended round the neck, for which there were other special decorations in the shape of gorgets and torques. In form they are identical with the nimbi on ancient carvings; and in the great majority of the oldest Byzantine pictures, similar ornaments surround the heads of the personages represented in scriptural pieces, or holy families. And, as many of these pictures are painted on panels, the glories, or nimbi, are generally plates of metal (usually silver gilt) fastened to the wood. There is a similar nimbus round the head of the chief figure in the Knockmoy fresco, described at page 316 of Vol. I. Montfaucon has figured many examples of half-moon-shaped head ornaments in use among the ancient Greeks and Romans; and in the Etruscan Collection at Berlin may be seen several bronze statuettes with this exact head-dress; in one of which (that of a female) a plait of hair is drawn across the front of the lunula, between it and the forehead.

We have no special reference to these ornaments in Irish history; but in the *Vision of Adamnan*** there is a passage that bears upon such a form of head-dress, where it refers to "the exceedingly large arch above the head of the Illustrious One, in his regal chair, like the adorned helmet, or the *Mind* of a king."† In one of the MS. copies of Cormac's Glossary, the article referred to is thus explained:—" A *mind* that used to

---

* See Mr. Eugene O'Curry's "Lectures on the Manuscript Materials of Ancient Irish History" for an account of this Tract, p. 424.

† Extract supplied by Mr. J. O'B. Crowe, who has also referred me to two passages in the *Leabhar na h- Uidhré*, in which the term *Mind* (pronounced *Meend*), and often spelled in " middle Irish" *Minn*, occurs, and bears a like signification to that given in the text.

be put upon the head of a soldier after the victory of conquest." In a fragment of a commentary on the Gospel of St. Mark, preserved in the University Library at Turin, and written by an Irish scribe in the eighth or ninth century, *mind* glosses the Latin word *Diadema*. In the *Leabhar na h-uidhré*, a MS. of the eleventh century, we read that, "once upon a time, at the great fair held at Tailten, in Meath, by the Gaels, when Diarmaid, son of Fergus Cerrbeoil, was King of Tara, the men of Eirinn were ranged upon benches, each according to his dignity or profession, or legitimacy, as had been the custom thitherto. And the women had a separate bench assigned them, along with the king's two wives, Mairenn Mael [Mairenn the Bald], and Mugain, the daughter of Concraid, son of Duach Donn, of Munster. Mugain harboured a great envy against Mairenn, because she herself was childless; and said to a satirical woman who was there, that she would give her any reward she demanded, if she would snatch the golden *minn* off the Queen's head. Now, Mairenn was without hair upon her head, so she always wore a queen's *minn* to conceal her defect. The woman then came to where Mairenn was, and importuned her for a gift. The queen said she had it not. You shall have this, then, said the satirist, pulling the *Cathbarr* [a helmet or decorated headdress] of gold off her head. 'May God and St. Ciaran protect me against this,' said Mairenn, placing her hand upon her head; and, lo! no person in the fair had time to look at her, until a flowing head of golden hair fell down to her shoulders."*

A few bronze lunulæ have been found in Scandinavia, and there is one plain gold specimen in the Museum of Copenhagen. The northern antiquaries consider them to have been ornaments for confining the hair.†

---

* Extract supplied by Mr. O'Curry.

† The Copenhagen *Haarsmykker*, or gold lunula, figured by Vilhelm Boye in his *Oplysense Fortegnelse*, of ornaments of precious metals, in 1859, is thin, narrow, quite plain, 7¼ inches broad, and greatly resembles No. 12 in the Royal Irish Academy's Collection, both in size and absence of ornament. See p. 3 of that work.

When Bishop Pococke, who first figured and described this form of gold ornament, wrote in the Archæologia, in 1773, he said, " many such have been occasionally found in Ireland; and among these some are flat and plain; others crimpled or folded like a fan."—Vol. ii., p. 36. Simon and Vallancey also refer to similar plaited crescents; the folding, however, was evidently not a portion of the original device, but merely done by the spoiler or the finder to lessen the bulk of the article. The lunula figured by Vallancey in the fourth volume of his *Collectanea*, is evidently copied (although without acknowledgment) from that published by Pococke, ten years previously.

The subjoined illustration is drawn from No. 6, a rather

Fig. 530. No. 6.

small, but very perfect and beautifully decorated specimen of lunular ornament, in which the terminal plates are oblong, instead of circular. It stands 7 inches high, measures 6⅞ across, and is 5⅛ in the clear, and 1⅜ deep in the widest portion at top. Its weight is but 18 dwts. 2 grs. It was procured with the Dawson Collection. The inner circle, or cut-out portion, probably made to fit the head of the individual for whom the lunula was originally designed, differs in each particular specimen; and in size and shape it bears no relation to the magnitude of the entire article, of which circumstance No. 5 is a good example.

By the following illustrations, which are all drawn the natural size, are presented the various forms of decoration employed by the early Irish gold-workers, and they probably followed in succession, if they were not contemporary with, the ornamentation used on the sepulchral urns. In Nos. 3, 4, 15, and 9, may be seen the rudest and simplest forms

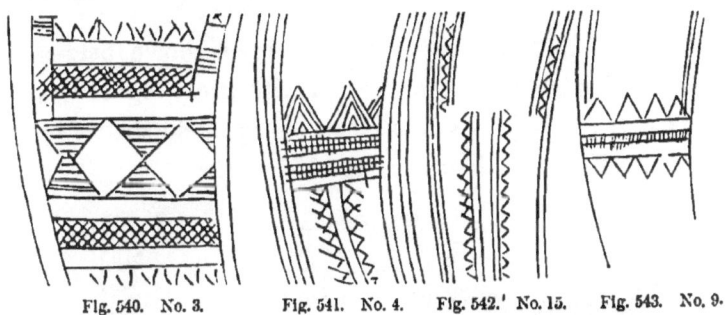

Fig. 540. No. 3.   Fig. 541. No. 4.   Fig. 542.' No. 15.   Fig. 543. No. 9.

of ornamentation, in which the lines are not very regular, and seldom quite straight or well defined, and the pattern is somewhat irregular, as figured above. The details of these specimens are given in the description of Case **A**. See page 17.

In figures 544, 545, and 546, from Nos. 8, 7, and 10, may be seen an advance in regularity of pattern, and greater precision of lining, especially in the last, where the pinking or angular-edged decoration is produced by a series of double lines meeting in the centre (the type of which may be seen in fig. 541, No. 4, of the foregoing cuts). In most others of this variety, the lines in the interspace run either across or perpendicularly. As already stated, at page 10, these short lines appear to have been produced by narrow chisel-faced punches of different lengths; but in most cases the prolonged lines were evidently made with the graver.

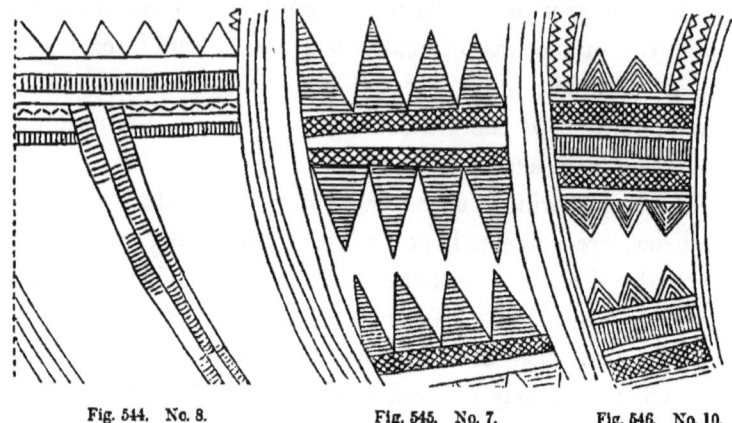

Fig. 544. No. 8.   Fig. 545. No. 7.   Fig. 546. No. 10.

In Fig. 547, drawn from No. 11, as shown below, the checkered work has been effected with great regularity, and the pattern resembles that on some of the shield-shaped bronze pins, see Fig. 448, Vol. I., page 557.

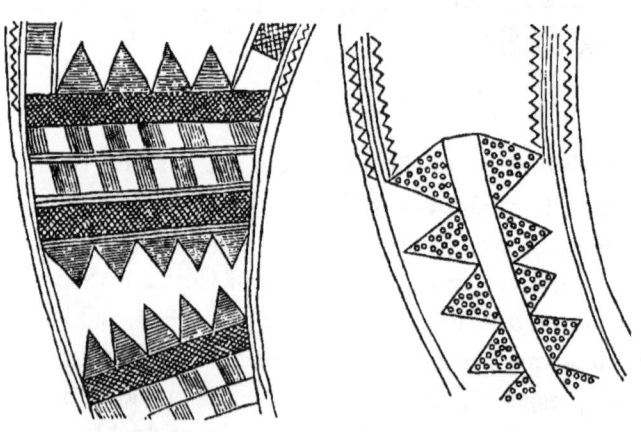

Fig. 547. No. 11.   Fig. 548. No. 13.

In No. 13, Fig. 548, a new style of ornament has been introduced, in which the pinking runs down each side of a double line, instead of across, as in all the other specimens;

CLASS V.—METALLIC MATERIALS: GOLD—LUNULÆ.

and the spaces within the outlines are filled up with a series of small circular punchings, like that in the bronze celt, No. 620, delineated at page 390, Vol. I.

Figure 549 represents a portion of the design on No. 5, the largest specimen of lunular ornament in the Collection. If brought out in colours, these various designs would have a very pleasing effect.

The foregoing collection may, in all probability, be received as the earliest specimens of lineal design in metal work which the remains of art in the British Isles afford. From the number found, it is manifest that this variety of ornament was in frequent use among the early Irish. In addition to the fifteen lunulæ in the Academy's Collection, we know of five others in private museums; there are three in the British Museum, which were found in Ireland; and we have reason to believe that several others are still unmelted, besides those mentioned by Simon, Pococke, Vallancey, Campbell, and other writers.

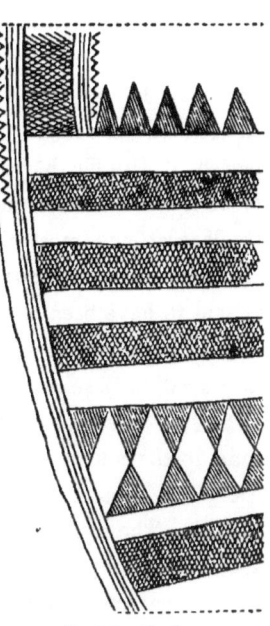

Fig. 549. No. 5.

The following list comprises the details of all the lunulæ in the Collection:—

Ground-Floor; Eastern Side.

Case **A** contains fifteen lunulæ, numbered from 1 to 15. No. 1, a small lunula, perfect in all respects, elaborately ornamented; measures 7¾ inches across, and is 5⅛ wide in the clear of the inner circle; it stands about 7½ inches high, and is 2⅜ deep in the broadest portion; weight, 1 oz. 10 dwt. 11 gr.—Purchased from a dealer. No. 2, ditto, large, perfect, slightly torn at upper and inner edges; figured and described as the typical specimen of this form of ornament at p. 10. No. 3, ditto, perfect, with the exception of the terminal cross plates, narrow; is $8\frac{1}{4}$ broad by 8 high, $6\frac{1}{2}$ in the clear, and 2 deep in the broadest portion; Wt., 2 oz. 2 dwt. Procured with the *Dawson* Collection. Ornament figured at p. 15. No. 4, one-half of a small lunula (completed with gold paper); measures $6\frac{3}{4}$ inches in extreme height; Wt., 10 dwt. 11 gr. Ornament figured at p. 15. Found with Nos. 8, 9, and 15, in hard gravel, apparently the remains of a *togher* or ancient road through a boggy field, in the parish of Dunfierth, barony of Carbury, and county of Kildare. Near it were found a quantity of bones of large ruminants. No. 5, the largest, and most highly ornamented specimen of lunula in the Collection; perfect, but divided into seven fragments, into which it is said to have been cut by the finder; it measures $11\frac{1}{8}$ inches broad, by $10\frac{3}{8}$ high, and is $4\frac{7}{8}$ deep in the widest portion. It is remarkably small in the clear, measuring but $5\frac{3}{4}$ inches across that portion; Wt., 4 oz. 3 dwt. 21 gr. Ornament figured at p. 17. Found near Athlone, in the county of Roscommon, and—*Presented in* 1842, *by Earl De Grey*, then Lord Lieutenant of Ireland. See Proc., vol. ii., p. 274. The square terminal plates were sold to the Academy subsequent to the presentation of the other portions. No. 6, a small, perfect, narrow lunula; figured and described at p. 14. No. 7, ditto, middle-sized, perfect; $7\frac{5}{8}$ by 7 inches broad, $5\frac{1}{2}$ in the clear, and $1\frac{5}{8}$ deep; Wt., 1oz. 9 gr. See Fig. 545, p. 16.—Purchased from a dealer. No. 8, ditto, perfect; large, broad, and rather wide at the opening; found with Nos. 4, 9, and 15. It was torn across at the widest portion, and the second part was not procured for many months after the first; when the parts were placed together, they were found to match. A small portion had been cut out of the upper edge of one fragment, to make a pig-ring, by the finder, who thought the metal was brass. This lunula has been restored, and in all probability now presents much of its original character. It measures $8\frac{7}{8}$ by $8\frac{1}{2}$ inches, is $6\frac{3}{4}$ wide in the clear, and $2\frac{3}{4}$ deep at top; Wt., 2 oz. 5 dwt. 1 gr. See Fig. 544, p. 16. No. 9, the left limb of a very small, narrow lunula, imperfect; finished out with gold paper; measures $7\frac{1}{2}$ inches long, and is 1 broad in the widest portion; Wt., 4 dwt. 2 gr. Found with Nos. 4, 8, and 15. Ornament figured at p. 15. No. 10, a lunula, perfect, complete; broad in lateral diameter of cut-out portion, and also wide in the opening at terminal plates; resembles No. 8; measures $7\frac{5}{8}$ inches wide, $7\frac{1}{8}$ high,

CLASS V.—METALLIC MATERIALS: GOLD—DIADEMS.

and $1\frac{3}{4}$ broad in widest portion; Wt., 1 oz. 3 dwt. See Fig. 546, p. 16. Obtained with the *Sirr* Collection, in the Catalogue of which it is stated to have been found in the county Galway. No. 11, ditto, perfect; broad at top; $7\frac{5}{8}$ inches wide by $7\frac{1}{2}$ high, $5\frac{1}{4}$ in the clear of the opening, and $2\frac{1}{2}$ deep in the widest portion; Wt., 1 oz. 7 dwt. 12 gr. Figured at p. 16.—Purchased from a dealer in 1852. No. 12, ditto, complete, but torn across the centre; narrow, quite unornamented; when it came into the Collection, it was crumpled or plated irregularly, as if to lessen its bulk; $7\frac{1}{2}$ inches wide, and the same high, $6\frac{1}{8}$ in the clear, and $1\frac{1}{4}$ deep at the top; terminal plates oblong; Wt., 18 dwt.—Purchased from a dealer in 1853. No. 13, both limbs of a highly ornamented lunula, deficient in the centre, but completed with gold paper; differs from all the others in the character of the punched ornament, figured and described at p. 16; measures 8 inches from out to out, each way, and is 6 wide in the clear of the opening; Wt., 14 dwt. 3 gr. Analyzed by Mr. J. W. Mallet, and found to consist of gold, 88·64; silver, 11·05; copper, 0·12. See Transactions, vol. xxii., No. 4, p. 315. No. 14, a perfect, very small horse-shoe-shaped lunula, quite unornamented; very wide in the opening, where it appears to have been stretched; measures $5\frac{3}{4}$ inches across, and 6 high, is $4\frac{5}{8}$ wide in the clear, and $1\frac{1}{8}$ broad in widest portion; Wt., 16 dwt. 16 gr.—*Dawson.* No. 15, the left limb of an ornamented lunula, wanting the terminal cross plate; it is about 9 inches long, and measures $1\frac{1}{8}$ wide at the broadest portion; Wt., 7 dwt. 19 gr. Found with Nos. 4, 8, and 9. See Fig. 542, p. 15.

DIADEMS, or TIARAS—in Irish, *Mind*, or *Minn*—of thin plates of gold, semi-oval in form, and most elaborately chased and embossed, have been frequently found in Ireland. There are at present five such ornaments in the Academy's Collection, arranged in Case B, at the eastern end of the Museum; and it may with safety be asserted that, both in design and execution, they are undoubtedly the most gorgeous and magnificent specimens of antique gold work which have as yet been discovered in any part of the world. Whether they were worn as the insignia of royalty, or formed portions of the head-dresses of Druid priests in Pagan times, is, in the present state of our knowledge, undetermined. The general design is the same in all, but differing slightly in the ornamental details in each specimen. Each diadem consists of a central crescentic plate, wide at top, and narrowing towards the ends, which are inserted into decorated circular bosses. These ornaments average eleven inches across, from out to out, and five in the clear of the open portion. In weight they vary from 4 to 16 ounces, and appear to have been placed in the erect position on the top of the head, like the lunulæ, but with the terminal decorated extremities coming down on each side, in front of, and partially covering the ears. How retained in position is uncertain. All the references to the *Mind* of the early Irish already cited at pages 12 and 13, in the description of the lunulæ, apply with even greater force to these diadems, of which the former were probably the precursors.

The semilunar nimbus, or oval part, is what is technically called "dished," or slightly concave posteriorly; and its ornamentation, which was evidently effected by hammering up, punching, or chasing on a mass of pitch or other yielding material, consists of a series of plain, polished, semicircular ribs, standing out in high relief, between which there are indented bands of rope-work, or rows of small circular elevations, all of the most elaborate and minute workmanship,—giving to the whole head-dress a most gorgeous effect.

Each shield-like boss is formed of a pair of thin convex plates, from two to four inches in diameter, and joined at their edges by a turn over in the posterior one, receiving and overlapping the thin edge of the anterior. In some cases, as in No. 17, this joining is further strengthened by a stout narrow rim of plain gold, which passes over and encircles the junction of both plates. The narrow terminations of the lunular portion pass in through slits in the posterior discs of the bosses, and are there fastened with gold wire twisted into a torque pattern; or, as in No. 17, with woollen thread encircled by a narrow spire of thin gold. Each anterior boss is elegantly chased, in a different style of ornament from the nimbus. The posterior plate or disc is also ornamented, but not so elaborately as that in front.

The first article of this description of which we have a notice is that truly grand diadem figured by General Vallancey, in vol. 4 of his *Collectanea de Rebus Hibernicis*, published in 1784, and which he supposed to be the celebrated collar of judgment worn by the renowned Brehon, Morann, in the reign of King Fearadach Finnfeachnach, who, according to the historian Keating, reigned A. D. 14.* It is said to have possessed the miraculous power of closing on the neck of the judge, if he pronounced an unrighteous sentence; or on that of the witness, if he swore falsely.† This so-called "*Iodhan Morain*" was found twelve feet deep in a bog in the county of Limerick, on the estate of W. Bury, and was in the possession of that gentleman's family in 1783. It was again figured in the *Vetusta Monumenta*, in 1819, when it was the property of the Earl of Charleville. See vol. v. Plate xxviii. Whether still in existence is uncertain. The engraving of it is $10\frac{3}{4}$ inches in diameter, and $3\frac{7}{8}$ across each boss. The article weighed twenty-two guineas, or 5 oz. 17 dwts. 8 gr., according to the weight of the guinea at that day,—being thus somewhat less than a third of No. 21, with which it has been frequently confounded. Vallancey also states that a similar article was found in the county of Longford, and sold for

---

* A. D. 15. In this reign lived Morann Mac Maein, son of Cairbre the Cat-headed, Chief Brehon of Ireland, who possessed the celebrated *Sin*, or chain, called "*Idh Morainn*," which it is said would contract round the neck of a guilty person. See *Leabhar Gabhala;* also notes to the Annals of the Four Masters, by Dr. O'Donovan, who says this chain is mentioned in several commentaries on the Brehon Laws.

† To the *Gearr Bearuigh*, or short crozier of St. Barry, still in the possession of the O'Hanley family, was attributed the like property; and it was placed round the neck, when used in swearing, in the counties of Roscommon and Longford, within the memory of the writer. See the author's Description of the *Mias-Tighearnain*, in the Trans. R. I. A., Vol. xxi., Part ii.

twenty-six guineas. Among the Irish articles in the Collection of Trinity College, there is a splendidly ornamented boss, 4⅜ inches wide, manifestly not belonging to any of those articles now known. (See a drawing thereof in Table 52 of the Portfolio of the Museum, and a cast of it in the Comparative Collection.) In 1749, a circular boss, 10 inches in diameter, with a portion of a fluted diadem attached to it by gold twist, was found in the bog of Cullen, county of Tipperary.* We have thus an account of no less than ten golden diadems, including the five perfect specimens, and a separate boss, now in the possession of the Royal Irish Academy.†

The three following woodcuts, Figs. 550, 551, and 552,

Fig. 550. No. 21.

afford typical illustrations of these diadems; and Figs. 553,

---

* See the Rev. Mr. Armstrong's communication to Governor Pownall, in the *Archæologia*, Vol. iii., p. 363, for an account of that and all the other gold articles discovered in Cullen Bog, from June, 1731, to the year 1771.

† In vol. iii. of the *Collectanea Antiqua* of Mr. C. Roach Smith, the late Crof-

554, and 555, represent the most remarkable forms of decoration on their lateral ornamented bosses. No. 21, Fig. 550, is the largest and most beautiful head-dress in the Collection. The gold of which it is composed is very red; and in style of ornament and character of boss, as well as in the manner of fastening, this article differs somewhat from the others. The arched or lunated portion consists of three elevated rolls, with rows of conical studs on each, four on the upper, and three on each of the two others. A very minute rope-shaped fillet occupies the sulci between each elevation. The edges, both externally and internally, are turned over stout twisted gold wires of the torque pattern. The narrow extremities terminate in strong and rather plain bosses, to the posterior plates of which they are fastened; not by wires or gold threads, as in each of the other specimens, but by the plates being cut in several places, and turned back upon the inside of the disc, and further strengthened by stout bands of gold bent round them. This joining, although firmly secured, does not, however, appear to have been soldered, except at one or two points. The discs are circular, and $2\frac{1}{2}$ inches wide; the posterior one is plain, smooth, massive, and concave; the anterior is flat, and decorated like the arched portion with two rows of small nail-headed elevations, surrounding a central umbo with a double edging. The goldsmith, in making this article, apparently first fastened the extremity of the arch to the posterior disc in the manner described above, and then attached to it the flat anterior plate by the overlapping of its edge. This ornament, which is quite complete, though fractured in two places, weighs altogether 16 oz. 10 dwts. 13 grs.; it stands $11\frac{1}{2}$ inches high, the same across, is 5 in the clear of the

---

ton Croker has figured a circular gold plate, embossed like the disc of a diadem, and which covered a similar article in copper. It was found in the county Cork; and if not a portion of a fibula, such as I have referred to at p. 557, Vol. I., it must have been the anterior plate of the lateral boss of a diadem.

opening, and 4½ deep at top, but narrows to 2 inches at each extremity. It was procured with the Sirr Collection, and is said to have been found in the county Clare.

No. 18, Fig. 551, here shown in perspective, is slightly defective at the upper edge; it was in two portions when presented for sale in 1856, and in mending, it has been slightly

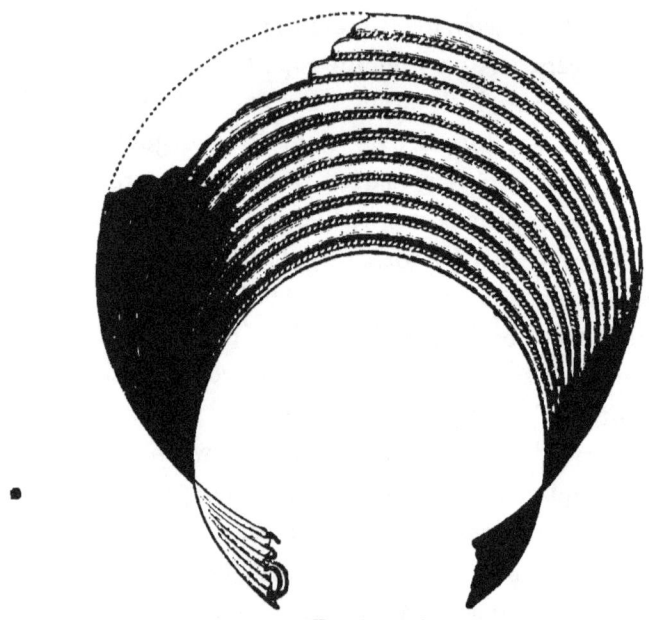

Fig. 551. No. 18.

contracted in the inner circle. It stands 8½ inches high, measures 10 wide, is 4½ across the open part, 4¼ deep in the broadest portion at top, and narrows to 2 at each extremity. It is formed of a very thin plate of gold, and weighs only 3 oz. 9 dwt. 23 gr. The ornamentation consists of eleven plain raised ribs, with twelve roped bars between. The edges are strengthened by a narrow hem or turn over of the metal. A torque wire of two strands, apparently the remains of its fastening to one of the lateral bosses, passes through a number of holes in one end. This article, which was found at Tory Hill, parish of Croom, county of Limerick, was purchased from a dealer.

No. 20, one of the handsomest and most perfect diadems in the Museum, formed of reddish gold, is here represented by Fig. 552. Its ornament consists of five plain, broad, ele-

Fig. 552. No. 20.

vated bands, between which are four large funiform decorations. A narrow roped fillet occupies the inner edge, and a double and more elevated one, the outer. Portions of both posterior discs of the terminal bosses, with radiating grooved lines, still remain attached to the ends of the arch. We also possess one of the anterior discs, shown below by Fig. 553. The entire article weighs 7 oz. 8 dwts. 1 gr.; it measures $10\frac{3}{4}$ inches high, is $10\frac{1}{4}$ wide, $4\frac{3}{4}$ in the clear, $4\frac{1}{4}$ deep at top, and $2\frac{1}{4}$ at each narrow end. The remarkably thin posterior discs are still attached by gold-wire threads to the plain ends of the arched or lunated portion, which pass into them, as shown in the foregoing cut. This diadem was procured with the Dawson Collection.*

The annexed illustration, drawn half-size, shows the remaining anterior disc of No. 20, which weighs but 4 dwt. 23 gr. It is flat, and composed of a very thin plate, most elaborately tooled, and hammered up into a high central umbo, surrounded by nine cones, each encircled with a series of minutely raised lines of the most delicate tracery. A transversely decorated bur or fillet surrounds the edge, and another of a like description encircles the central elevation.

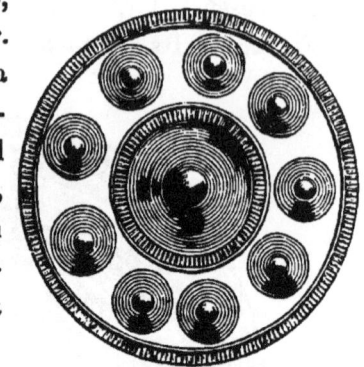

Fig. 553. No. 20.

Figure 554, also drawn half-size from the large scutiform anterior disc of one of the bosses of No. 17, is most curiously and elaborately decorated with two rows of conical studs, surrounding the central umbo, each row enclosed within a double raised fillet, resembling twisted wire. The umbo itself is encircled by a series of minutely raised lines, from which it is separated by another torque-shaped fillet. This exceedingly thin convex plate is attached to the posterior disc by a turn over of the latter, and the union is rendered more secure by a narrow hoop of gold, which overlaps the marginal joining, and strengthens the whole;

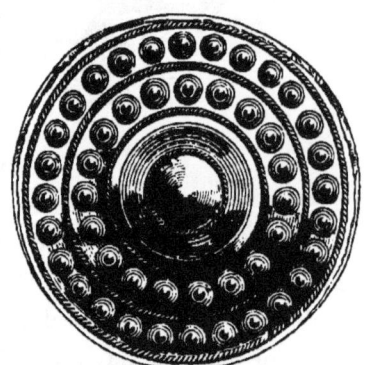

Fig. 554. No. 17.

---

* Now that a taste has sprung up for personal decorations of the same pattern as the ancient Irish jewellery, it is matter of surprise that head-dresses similar to our ancient *Minds* have not been introduced.

the ends of the hoop are not soldered at the point of junction. The annexed cut, Figure 555, is a back view of the posterior disc of the same left boss, and shows the most highly decorated example of that portion of the *Mind* in the Collection, as also the manner in which the termination of the lunated part passes into the transverse slit, where it is fastened above and below the line of junction. The character and design of the ornament is of a piece with that

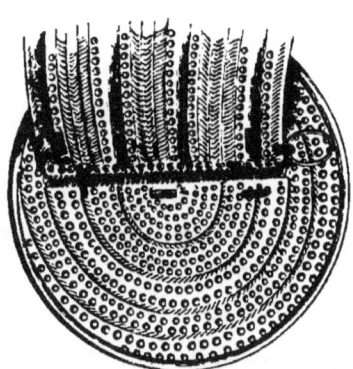

Fig. 555. No. 17.

employed in the arch and the anterior disc, but the studs and intervening rope-work are more minute. Where the end of the diadem overlapped and concealed a portion of the posterior plate, the latter is plain, showing that even in these early days of art, labour was economized. A broad funiform band margins the transverse slit for the reception of the end of the arch, which is there decorated with a row of small nail-headed projections, while the other ornaments of this portion, as seen from the obverse, are indented. Above the line where the end of the plate passes into the boss, may be seen three perpendicular, and below it two longitudinal stitches. Some of these sewings are effected by slight square wire; but in others the fastenings are composed of fine woollen thread, round which is twisted spirally a thin flat strip of gold, as already described. That is in all probability the oldest specimen of woollen cordage now in existence in Ireland, and very likely dates from a period anterior to the knowledge of either silk, hemp, or flax, in this country. To the lower concave edge of the arch is attached, by a staple, a small oval ring, evidently for the purpose of fastening it to the head; but neither in these fastenings, nor in any other part of this ornament, can be perceived the slightest trace of soldering; and it may fairly be presumed that, if that art was known to the fabricator, it would have been employed, instead of the wire-sewing already described. The other termination of the arch is attached to the posterior disc of the boss, by no less than eleven stitches.

The diadem, No. 17, to which these bosses belong, is very perfect, and most elaborately chased; it weighs only 4 oz. 6 dwts. 2 grs.; and measures 10½ inches across the widest portion, 5 in the clear of the open part; is 3½ deep at top, and 3 at each extremity. The plate is thin, and the ornamentation is formed of four plain elevated narrow ribs, between each of which is an embossed fillet, consisting of two rows of raised studs, with three coils of rope-work between them, as seen in this cut. There is only one row of studs, and one rope-

Fig. 556. No. 17.

like fillet at each edge, which is turned in all round, to remove the sharpness, and strengthen the plate. It was found in 1836, lying on the gravel, four feet deep, beneath the surface of a turf bog, on the lands of Burrisnoe, to the eastern side of Benduff Mountain, county of Tipperary, and was procured by the Academy along with the Dawson Collection.

The following detailed list enumerates all the articles of this description in the Museum:—

Case **B** contains five golden diadems, and a fragment of a sixth, numbered from 16 to 21. No. 16 is a splendid golden diadem, of a semilunar form, perfect, with the exception of the boss on the right side; it is highly ornamented, with seven plain raised ribs, and eight indented bars, each bar consisting of three rows, the oblique roping of which is so regular as to appear to have been effected by machinery. It is semi-ovoid in form, and composed of a very thin plate of gold, but with the edges overlapping, to give it stability. Each narrow extremity ends in a plain, very thin plate, which passes through a slit in the back disc of the terminal boss on each side. The arch is slightly dished, and measures 10¼ inches from out to out of the lateral diameter, and is 5½ in the clear of the opening. It is

CLASS V.—METALLIC MATERIALS: GOLD—DIADEMS. 29

$4\frac{1}{4}$ deep at the top, and $2\frac{1}{2}$ at each boss. There is only one anterior boss remaining, that on the left side. It is highly ornamented, like a shield, with a central conical umbo, and fourteen minor elevations, surrounded by six circles. It is of still thinner gold than the body of the ornament, and measures $2\frac{7}{8}$ inches across. A series of small conical projections surround the edge, within which there is a double funiform elevation, similar to that in the diadem. Internal to that line there are fourteen cones, as stated above. Still, within these is a double twisted elevation, and yet more towards the centre, a series of oblique radiating raised lines; then a double rope, then five raised circular lines, like those round the umbo, within which is a single rope, encircling the central elevation. This plate was fastened upon the posterior disc by an overlapment of the latter, as in the joining of modern tin-ware. It weighs 3 dwt. 22 gr.: and measures $2\frac{3}{4}$ inches across; the whole diadem now weighs 4 oz. 5 dwt. 5 gr.

The posterior concave members of each boss remain *in situ*, and are decorated with five rows of circular conical knobs, smaller than those on the anterior side; each row divided by a double roping. It is cut transversely, to admit the small end of the lunular portion of the diadem, which then passes down into the hollow between the two discs. This slit is margined by a double roping, to correspond with the cross roping embossed on the reverse side of the small end of the diadem, precisely like Figure 555, from which it is difficult to distinguish it, except by the size. The upper portion of this posterior plate, which is concealed by the diadem, is plain; thus we see that labour was economized in early times. The lunular portion was fastened to the boss by square wire, twisted into the torque pattern, three above in line with the transverse funiform decoration, and two below the transverse cut in the boss. This ornament was found in a bog, one spade's depth under the surface, in the parish of Ardcroney, near Nenagh, county of Tipperary. No. 17, another diadem of the same size as the foregoing, but with less elevated chasing, and having larger bosses; it is slightly imperfect on left outer edge; plate thinner than that in No. 16; both anterior discs of bosses remain, right posterior disc broken; both sides of the left boss have been figured at pp. 26, 27; the diadem itself is described at length in the text, and a portion figured at p. 28. No, 18, the golden diadem, figured and described at p. 24. No 19, the anterior disc of the lateral boss of a diadem, much larger than any other in the Collection; it is more convex than usual in such articles; measures $4\frac{1}{2}$ inches across, and weighs 16 dwt. 2 gr. The decoration is ruder than in any of the other specimens, and consists of a number of minute conical projections, with a donble circle externally. It formed a portion of the old Collection of the Academy. See Mallet's Analysis:—No. 6, gold, 81·10; silver, 12·18; copper, 5·94; lead, 0·28. Trans. R. I. A., vol. xxii., p. 315. No. 20, the splendid gold diadem, figured and described at pp. 25, 26. No. 21, the largest and heaviest gold diadem in the Collection; it is figured and described at p. 22.

GORGETS, or NECK-COLLARS.—While the precise use and mode of wearing the lunulæ, or moon-shaped plates, are questions still open to discussion, no doubt can exist as to the object of the articles termed "Gorgets;" for an exactly similar piece of decorative defence was worn by modern soldiers within the last few years.* Indeed, it may be fairly asserted that no article of ancient personal decoration has descended to our own time with less alteration than this; and even when no longer considered useful for defence, small figurative or emblematic gorgets, of gilt brass, were suspended by ribbons (furnished with rosettes) from the necks of infantry officers, of which there is a specimen in the Comparative Collection of the Academy's Museum. It is only within the last few years that any of those ancient gold gorgets have been discovered; and as yet the only specimens to be seen in the public antiquarian museums of Europe are those in the Irish Academy's Collection.† They were all found together, in March, 1854, with a vast number of golden antiquities, in

---

* We have no ancient Irish name that specially applies to gorget. *Muin-tore*, or neck-torque, was probably a generic term for several varieties of twisted neck ornaments, but is certainly not applicable to the smooth, curved gorget.

† A sixth gorget, weighing 4 oz. 13 dwt., was also found; it was purchased by the late Lord Londesborough.

CLASS V.—METALLIC MATERIALS: GOLD—GORGETS. 31

making the Limerick and Ennis Railway, through the townland of Mooghaun North, in the parish of Tomfinlough, near Quin, and not far from Newmarket-on-Fergus, in the county of Clare, and form a part of the great "Clare Find," a portion of which was purchased by means of a Government grant and subscriptions from some members of the Academy. It is said that no less than £3000 worth of gold articles were discovered on that occasion. Besides these gorgets, there were found an immense number of rings and armillæ, several fibulæ, and some small torques, the whole placed together in a small stone chamber made for their reception, immediately beneath the surface, in dry alluvial soil.

The Rev. Dr. Todd, then Secretary to the Academy, brought all the circumstances of this most remarkable discovery under the notice of the stated meeting, held on the 26th of June following, and exhibited five gorgets, two necktorques, two unwrought ingots, and no less than one hundred and thirty-seven rings and armillæ; the total weight of which was 174 oz. 11 dwt. 7 grs. It is to be lamented that that most valuable communication has not been preserved in our Proceedings; but the author having generously placed his MS. notes at our disposal, we are here enabled to supply a more authentic account of this discovery than has yet appeared. There was a small mound of earth over the little stone chamber in which the gold ornaments were found: the rings and torques were twisted together, and covered on the outside by the gorgets. This hoard, which was evidently hidden in haste, was manifestly the spoil of a battle, foray, or plundering; but the depositors never returned for it. The locality is not more than a quarter of a mile from one of the largest earthen forts in Ireland, and lies north-east of the demesne of Dromoland, the property of Lord Inchiquin, a most remarkable fort,* which was, in all probability, the

---

* See Ordnance Map of Clare, sheet 42. The fort is not named on the map, but a writer in the "Munster News" of the day stated that it was called Laungagh.

theatre of many a conflict in early times. This portion of the ancient territory of Thomond was the scene of a great struggle between the Norsemen and the native clans of the O'Briens. The ancient tract on the Wars of the Gail (i. e. the Danes) with the Gaedhil, or Irish, now in process of publication, contains several notices of these conflicts, of which the following is a summary:—

" Mahon, brother of Brian, makes peace with the Danes. But Brian, son of Kennedy [afterwards called Brian Boroihme] was not pleased with this peace, but prepared to inflict all the evils in his power on the Danes; and although all others sat idle, Brian would not. He retired with vigorous youths of the Dalcais into the woods and wildernesses of Thomond, and immediately commenced hostilities against the Danes. They erected huts and encampments in the forests and solitudes of Hi Bloid* [the very district in which these gold ornaments were found], and laid waste all between Loch Derg and the River Fergus, and from Echtge to Tradree.† The Danes enclosed the whole of Tradree with a wall of fortification; but Brian continued to harass them, and to cut them off in small parties without number, at the same time that he was so reduced himself that at one time he had but fifteen youths to follow him." Soon afterwards Brian and Mahon gained a great battle over the Danes at Laigh, in Tradree. "They plundered Finn Inis, and Inis Mor, and Inis da Dhromin, and the other islands of the river, and every place that held the wives and children of the Danes; and

---

* "The descendants of Blod, the eldest son of Cas, ancestor of the O'Briens, inhabited the region from them called *Hy-mBloid.* The territory is indicated . . in the east of the county of Clare, and diocese of Killaloe."—See Historical Memoir of the O'Briens, by John O'Donoghue, A. M. Dublin, 1860: p. 10 and note.

† Echtge, now Slieve Aughty, on the confines of Clare and Galway. Tradree, or Tradraighe, is the name of a deanery in Clare, comprising nine parishes, among which Tomfinlough, in which the gold was found, is one, as also the island of Inisda-dhrom, in the Shannon, at the mouth of the River Fergus. See Annals of the Four Masters, O'Donovan's translation, and notes.

CLASS V.—METALLIC MATERIALS: GOLD—GORGETS.   33

there was much of gold and other wealth in these islands and fortifications."—MS. in Trin. Coll., H. 2, 17, pp. 34, 47, 61.

It is, therefore, not improbable that this hoard of gold, the spoils of the Irish by the Danes, who are frequently described by our ancient writers as "Exactors of Rings," may have been deposited by that people before their final rout by the victor of Clontarf. Had it been hidden by the Irish, the knowledge of the circumstance would, most likely, have been preserved, and it would not have remained unsought for or undiscovered for upwards of eight centuries.*

The British Museum and several private Collections have been enriched from that "Find;" but there is reason to fear that a large portion of it found its way to the smelting pot.

The five gorgets have been arranged at the top of Case C.

Fig. 557.   No. 25.

No. 25, figured above, is the largest and most perfect. It measures 21 inches along its convex margin, is 7½ across the

---

* For further notices of the "Clare find," see Proc. R. I. A., Vol. vi., pp. 113 and
VOL. II.   D

widest part, and 5½ in the clear. It is formed of a semi-oval stout plate of gold, 2¼ inches wide, measured over the broadest part of the convexity, and is ¾ of an inch in the opening between the terminal cups. These latter do not present parallel faces; but when the article is laid on the flat, each looks backwards, and slightly downwards. Their necks are decorated in front with a highly engraved pattern, consisting of encircling fillets above and below a herring-bone pattern, as shown in the annexed cut. It weighs 7 oz. 3 dwt. 12 gr. As, owing to its shape and material, it is very flexible, it can be easily passed round the neck by bringing one end forwards and pressing the other backwards.

Fig. 558. No. 25.

The discovery of these undoubted gorgets or neck collars strengthens our belief that the lunulæ were intended for the head, as already stated at page 12. The foregoing description of No. 25 applies to the other four, the details of which are given in the description of Case **D**, at page 41. Without any exact knowledge on the subject of the ornaments and costume of the Danes, at the time of their occupation of some of our cities, it is impossible to form an opinion as to the character of the "collar of gold which Malachy won from the proud invader;" but it is worthy of remark that the principal articles of gold in the Copenhagen Museum are massive collars, round in section, some hinged behind, and overlapping in front.

BEADS and NECKLACES—in Irish, *Fiam muinche*—either of gold alone or gold and amber, were not uncommon in Ireland. The most remarkable and unique objects of this description

---

124; also an article by the Rev. James Graves, in the Kilkenny Archæological Journal, Vol. iii., p. 181; and the late Mr. Crofton Croker's paper in the *Collectanea Antiqua*, p. 230; together with the newspapers of the period.

All the articles from the Clare find now in the Collection of the Academy were procured through the instrumentality of the Rev. Doctor Todd, Charles Haliday, Esq., and Christopher Fleming, M. D.

are the eleven hollow balls, or large globular beads, which were found by a peasant in a potatoe field near Carrick-on-Shannon, in the county of Leitrim, in 1834, and of which there are now seven in the Collection, arranged in Case C, and numbered from 28 onwards. This illustration represents these

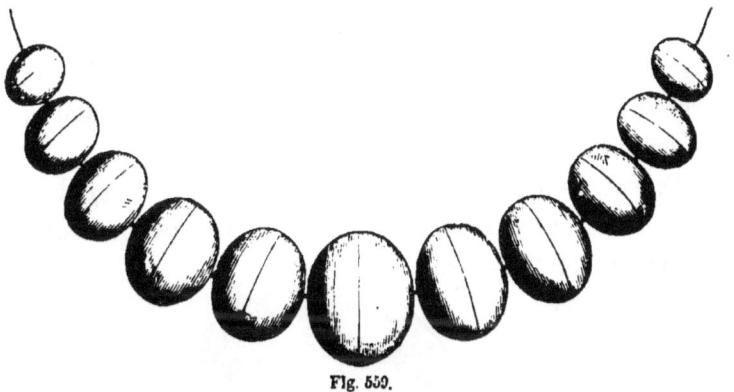

Fig. 559.

objects in their entirety, as they originally came into the possession of Mr. West, of this city, before they were distributed amongst several collections prior to the formation of the Academy's Museum; and the annexed figure, drawn from No. 31, represents one of these articles separately. Each ball is slightly compressed laterally, and is formed of two hemispheres of very thin gold plate, so made as to join with the greatest accuracy, and to overlap for about the sixteenth of an inch. They

Fig. 560. No. 31.

were then soldered at the extreme edges, so slightly, yet intimately, that the uniting material can only be discovered with the aid of a lens. On the flattened side of each of these balls there is an aperture somewhat less than a quarter of an inch wide, with an everted lip, as if to prevent fraying of the band on which they were strung. Those seven hollow balls now in the Collection vary in size from $2\frac{3}{4}$ to $3\frac{7}{8}$ inches in the greatest diameter, and in weight from 1 oz. 8 dwt. 20 gr., as in the least, No. 28, to No. 31A, which is 2 oz. 7 dwt. 7 gr. The entire set weighed 20 oz. 8 dwt. Several are now much battered, but when found it is said that they were smooth and perfect. It is apparent that a necklace formed of these eleven balls must have descended as low as the breast. Research does not aid our inquiries as to what class they were worn by, whether chieftain, Druid-priest, or king, but their ostensible use was that of a necklace of the largest and most gorgeous description.*

One of the most elegant forms of ancient Irish gold ornament is that here represented, the actual size, both on the flat and in section, and which may be termed the *Double Conical Bead*. It is formed of two very thin conical plates, most elaborately decorated with a series of minute concentric depressions and eleva-

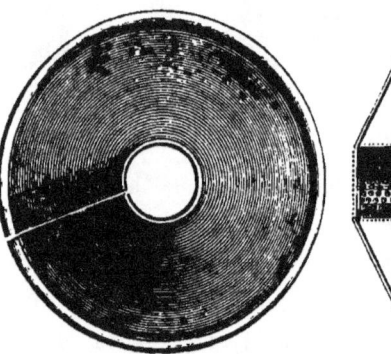

Fig. 561. No. 49.   Fig. 562. No. 49.

tions, and open at one side, but for what purpose it is now difficult to determine.† In each of these plates there is a large central aperture, through which passed a cylindrical pipe, ¾ inch long and ⅜ wide, punched all over from within outwards, and which was fastened to the conical sides by an interlapping edge, as shown by Fig. 562. The outer approximated edges of the discs were encircled with a stout plain rim, or overlapping hoop, which held them together, like that seen in the boss of the diadem, No. 17, described at page 26. It

---

* See The Dublin Penny Journal, Vol. iii., p. 144.

† The late Crofton Croker, in his learned article on Irish gold, in C. Roach Smith's *Collectanea Antiqua*, Vol. iii., p. 136, supposed them to be Bullæ.

weighs 8 dwt. 2 gr. There are the remains of four such beads of different sizes in Case C, Nos. 48 to 51, the largest of which, No. 49, is that figured on the opposite page.* Nos. 41 to 47, in the same Case, are a row of cylindrical Beads, corresponding in every respect with the tube or ferule still remaining in the double cylindrical ornament just alluded to; and, although they were found with the amber necklace discovered at Cruttenclough, near Castlecomer, county of Kilkenny, and now in the Academy's Collection (see Rail-case E), they were probably originally bushings or centre tubes for conical beads.

Two other forms of small conical beads are here shown, the natural size. Fig. 563 represents a small embossed bead, composed of two cones joined in the centre: it forms a portion of a necklace of seven similar hollow beads, numbered from 34 to 40, in Case C, each weighing from 9 to 11 grains. Fig. 564 is drawn from one of a series of seven similar double beads, numbered from 52 to 58, each consisting of two chalice-shaped portions, joined in the centre, decorated with transverse embossed lines; and having small trumpet-mouthed extremities. The average weight of each bead is 1 dwt. 8 gr. The necklace to which this article belongs was procured with the Sirr Collection; and No. 35 forms a part of that which was found at Cruttenclough, referred to above. This latter belonged to Dean Dawson.

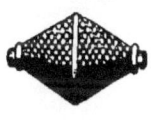
Fig. 563. No. 35.

Fig. 564. No. 52.

EAR-RINGS—in Irish, *Unasca*—are well represented by the

---

* In the collection of drawings now in my custody, made by G. Beranger at the end of the last century, and to which reference has been made at p. 439, Vol, I., there is a coloured illustration of a large and very perfect double conical bead of this description, which measures 2¼ inches in diameter. Except in size, the only difference between it and that figured above consists in a small double-roped ornament along the parallel edges of the transverse joining of the side plates.

gold articles in the Collection, and illustrated by the three following figures, drawn the actual size, from Nos. 62, 63, and 66, in Case C. Each ring is disunited, but was probably closed after having been passed through a hole in the lobe of the auricle. No. 62 is a close funiform, or torque-shaped ear-ring, one of four similar in pattern, with small plain ends.

Fig. 565. No. 62. Fig. 566. No. 63. Fig. 567. No. 66.

It weighs 3 dwt. 4 gr. No. 63, Fig. 566, is a very beautiful massive ear-ring of the torque pattern, formed of four flat narrow fillets, joined at their inner edges, like the great Tara torque, No. 192, in Case E. These twisted bands terminate in circular collars, from which the plain round ends proceed. It weighs 12 dwt. 9 gr., and forms one of a pair said to have been found near Castlerea, county of Roscommon, and procured with the Sirr Collection. Figure 567, No. 66, is of a totally different character from either of the foregoing, and consists of a number of transverse rolls or elevations, with a wheel-like ornament in the centre. It weighs 9 dwt. 4 gr.

LONGITUDINAL GOLD PLATES,—plain and decorated, some long and narrow, as No. 82, Fig. 568; and others short and broad, as No. 75, Fig. 569; or with central loops, as No. 73, Fig. 570,—have been frequently found in Ireland. There are nine such articles arranged beneath the balls and beads in Case C, illustrative examples of which are afforded by the subjoined engravings. Their use has not with certainty been determined; but in all likelihood the elongated specimens were employed as fillets or forehead-bands, for confining the hair, and the shorter ones may have hung over the brow. Figure 568 represents, the actual size, a portion of No. 82, which is 8¼ inches long. The ornament, which is in relief, and would appear to have been struck with a die or stamp, is more of the Scandinavian than the Irish pattern. The plate

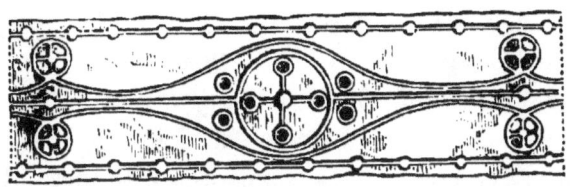

Fig. 568. No. 82.

is very thin, and weighs only 5 dwt. It was found at Lambay Island, in Dublin Bay; and from the statement of a sword being found along with it, it has been conjectured that it formed part of the decoration of that weapon; but the account afforded by the finder is not very clear as to the circumstance of the discovery.

Figure 569, drawn one-half size from No. 75, shows a thin decorated plate, one of four similar articles, each with ten transverse, raised, triple bars; and which were either worn in the hair, on the forehead, or attached to the dress. It weighs 1 dwt. 17 gr. Figure 570, No. 73, is a plain thin plate of gold, with a hook at top, probably for a like purpose. It weighs 3 dwt. 17 gr. There are two such plates in the Collection.* See details of Case C, at page 44.

Fig. 569. No. 75.

---

* Golden fillets, or hair-bands, were not uncommon in Ireland; one of the most beautiful is that recently described by Mr. Windele in the Ulster Journal of Archæology, Vol. ix., part 33, for January, 1861. See an account of another similar hairband in the Kilkenny and South-East of Ireland Archæological Journal, vol. i., No. 8, p. 361.

No. 75, Fig. 569, together with Nos. 71 and 72, was found during the arterial drainage operations, in 1852, in the bed of a stream in the townland of Belleville, parish of Kilmore, county of Cavan, and were—*Presented by the Board of Works.*

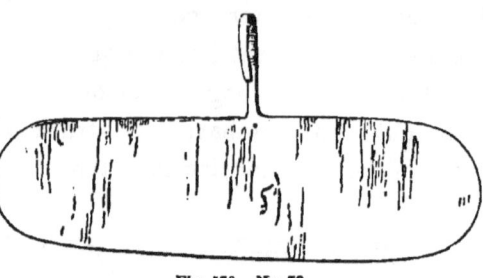

Fig. 570. No. 73.

BREAST-PINS and BROOCHES of gold—in Irish, *Dealg Oir*—are rare, especially in comparison with those of bronze and silver, and were probably not in use in those early days when the diadems, hair-plates, lunulæ, torques, gorgets, necklaces, and double-headed mammillary fibulæ, were the chief personal metallic ornaments. But some of the most elaborately wrought bronze, silver, and findyuin, or white metal, brooches, and forehead decorations, were partially covered with plates of gold, as already alluded to at pages 354 and 557, Vol. I. These gold-plated articles will be again referred to in the description of the articles of silver. A gold ring-fibula of the bronze and silver pattern, and styled the "Dalriada Brooch," was found some years ago in the neighbourhood of Coleraine, county of Antrim, and figured and described in the Ulster Journal of Archæology, vol. iv., page 1. In workmanship and style of art it is, however, much inferior to many of our bronze and silver ring-brooches, and is probably of as recent a date as the twelfth century.[*]

---

[*] See Proc. R. I. A., vol. vi., p. 302. Another golden ring-brooch, found in Ireland, has been described in the Archæological Journal, vol. xi., p. 285. For the Irish names of breast-pins and brooches, see p. 554, Vol. I. of this Catalogue.

When the poet Aithirne visited the county of Carlow, as related in the *Forbais Edair*, he procured a beautiful gold brooch, and carried it with him to Ulster. See the curious account of this antique in Mr. O'Curry's "Lectures," p. 268, already referred to at p. 12. In 1801, the Royal Dublin Society purchased an antique gold fibula, which was found in the county of Fermanagh. See Proc. of that body.

CLASS V.—METALLIC MATERIALS: GOLD—BREAST-PINS. 41

The few breast-pins belonging to the Royal Irish Academy, arranged in Case C, from Nos. 83 to 88, are comparatively modern. They consist of small ring-brooches, three of which bear inscriptions, and the two very light, elegant pins shown, the exact size, by the accompanying illustrations. The shorter, No. 83, Fig. 571, has a double torque-pattern ring; and the long pin of No. 84, Fig. 572, has a drill-shaped ferule and cross-bar at the upper part. Its ring is plain and unclosed. The former article weighs 2 dwt. 12 gr.; and the latter 3 dwt. 14 gr.

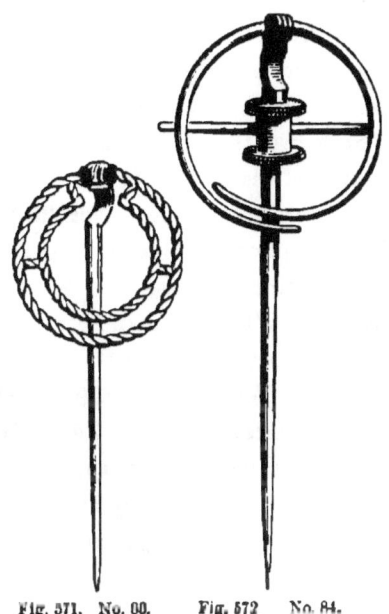

Fig. 571. No. 80.   Fig. 572. No. 84.

The following is a detailed list of the seventy-eight articles attached to Case C:—

Case C, on the eastern ground-floor, contains a series of decorative articles—Gorgets, Balls, Beads, Necklaces, Forehead-bands, Plates, Pins, Brooches, Ear-rings, and Armillæ—numbered from 22 to 99. No. 22 is a small gold gorget, slightly imperfect at the extremities, flattened, and much battered; has a hole, apparently ancient, in one end; measures along its convex edge $16\frac{1}{2}$ inches; weight, 2 oz. 4 dwt. 19 gr.; found, with Nos. 23 to 27, and many other specimens of antique manufactured gold, among the great "Clare Find," described at p. 31. No. 23, a perfect gorget, of medium size, nearly circular, narrow, slightly cracked on inner edge; terminations small, flat, and undecorated; $6\frac{1}{4}$ inches wide, 5 in the clear, 1 across broadest part of turned-in edges, and $\frac{1}{2}$ between the terminal enlargements; Wt. 4 oz. 4 dwt. 4 gr. No. 24, a small, perfect gorget, thin, broad, and flat, partially bent and disfigured; terminations button-shaped; measures $5\frac{1}{4}$ inches across, 4 in the clear, and $\frac{1}{4}$ between ends; Wt. 2 oz. 8 dwt. 17 gr. No. 25, the largest and most perfect gorget in the Collection, figured and described as the type of its class at pp. 33 and 34. No. 26, a very perfect narrow gorget, more oval than the others; terminations slightly decorated with the graver, but ornament rude and irregular; ends button-shaped and slightly convex; $6\frac{1}{4}$ inches wide, $4\frac{3}{8}$ in the clear, and $1\frac{1}{4}$ across opening; but the aperture seems to have been widened; Wt. 6 oz. 8 dwt. 19 gr. Found, together with the four foregoing, in the county of Clare. See p. 34. No. 27, a massive gold ring, figured and described at p. 46. Nos. 28 to 33, a row of seven hollow gold balls of different sizes, varying in diameter from $2\frac{3}{4}$ to $3\frac{7}{8}$ inches, and described at p. 35. No. 28, a hollow ball, the smallest and most battered; Wt. 1 oz. 8 dwt. 20gr.; purchased from Mr. West. No. 29, ditto, in better preservation, and somewhat larger; $2\frac{7}{8}$ inches in diameter; Wt. 1 oz. 9 dwt. 9 gr. (Dawson). No. 30, ditto, larger, much battered; Wt. 2 oz. 7 dwt. 7 gr. (Dawson). No. 31, ditto, the largest and most perfect specimen; $3\frac{7}{8}$ inches in greatest diameter across joining. See Fig. 560, p. 35. No. 31A, the most perfect specimen in the set, $3\frac{6}{8}$ inches in diameter; Wt. 2 oz. 7 dwt. 7 gr.; procured while this page was correcting. No. 32, ditto, in tolerable preservation, but somewhat more flattened at the ends than any of the others; Wt. 2 oz. 8 gr. (Sirr). No. 33, ditto, in tolerable preservation, but larger than the corresponding one on the opposite side; Wt. 1 oz. 17 dwt. 13 gr. (Sirr).

Nos. 34 to 40, a row of seven small, hollow, double conical beads, about half an inch long each, varying in weight from 9 to 11 grains, and together amounting to 2 dwt. 22 gr. One of these is figured and described at p. 37. Nos. 41 to 47, a row of seven tubular beads, embossed with different patterns, each about $\frac{9}{10}$ inch long, and weighing from 5 to 7 grains; together amounting to 1 dwt. 18 gr. They, in all probability, originally formed the tubes of large, flat, double, conical beads, such as those described in the next lot, and one of which is figured at p. 36. These beads, with those previously described, are said to have formed part of an amber necklace, now in Railcase **E**, in Eastern Gallery, and found at Cruttenclough, near Castlecomer, county of Kilkenny.

Nos. 48 to 51, although of different sizes, and in great diversity of preservation, evidently belong to the same variety of ornament, the type of which is represented by Fig. 561, p. 36. No. 48, a compressed gold bead, ½ inch in diameter, formed of two conical portions, originally joined round a tube in the centre, and open at the side; Wt. 2 dwt. 19 gr. Purchased from a dealer. No. 49, ditto, large, figured and described at p. 36. No. 50, ditto, of very fine thin gold; although somewhat smaller, it is still more perfect than the foregoing, and is most elaborately tooled in concentric circles on the sides; 1½ inch in diameter, and ⅝ across central tube; Wt. 5 dwt. 2 gr. No. 51, a small conical bead, now flattened and horseshoe-shaped; minutely decorated on side-face; something more than ¾ inch wide; Wt. 20 gr. Nos. 52 to 58, a row of seven thin, embossed, chalice-shaped gold beads, a typical specimen of which is figured and described at p. 37. Each is about 1 inch long, and weighs from 1 dwt. 4 gr. to 1 dwt. 10 gr. (Sirr). No. 59, a torque-shaped, penannular ear-ring, with small plain ends; about ¾ of an inch in diameter; Wt. 1 dwt. 6 gr. No. 60, ditto; ⅞ inch wide in opening; Wt. 1 dwt. 1 gr. No. 61, ditto; thicker; 1 inch in diameter; Wt. 2 dwt. 15 gr. No. 62, ditto; Wt. 3 dwt. 4 gr. These four twisted ear-rings were procured with the Dawson Collection. The last is figured and described at p. 38. No. 63, the large torque ear-ring, figured and described at p. 38. No. 64, ditto, apparently the match of the foregoing, but somewhat lighter, and differing slightly in the form of the shoulder and collar; 1½ inch wide; ·Wt. 11 dwt. 20 gr. Found at Castlereagh, county of Roscommon (Sirr). No. 65, ditto, but smaller and slighter; wants the collars at extremities of torque portion; 1⅛ inch wide; Wt. 5 dwt. 8 gr. Found in the county Meath (Sirr). No. 66, an ear-ring of a different pattern to foregoing, figured and described at p. 38. No. 67, a small ring-pendant, with a hollow ball attached to it by a loop, probably a portion of an ear-ring; Wt. 13 gr. Nos. 68 and 69, in two parts, a golden tassel pendant from a loop, probably part of an ear-ring; 1 inch long; Wt. 2 dwt. 3 gr. No. 70, the fragment of a gold ornament, consisting of a central stem, with wire-work like that in a whip-handle, rising into three bars round it; probably part of an armlet; it appears to have been cut across with a sharp tool; 1 inch long; Wt. 6 dwt. 1 gr. No. 71, a thin gold plate, 3¼ inches long; decorated; Wt. 1 dwt. 13 gr.; found with Nos. 72 and 75. No. 72, ditto, somewhat larger, but torn across the centre; ornamented similar to foregoing, with marginal and transverse lines in two sets; measures $4\frac{1}{10}$ inches by $1\frac{1}{8}$; Wt. 2 dwt. 5 gr. No. 73, ditto, plain, with a loop at top; figured and described at p. 40. No. 74, ditto, plain; 5 inches long, and $1\frac{1}{2}$ wide; Wt. 4 dwt. 3 gr. No. 75, a thin plate, similar to No. 71. See Fig. 569, p. 39. No. 76, ditto, larger, corresponding to No. 72, on opposite side of Case, with transverse decorative bars, and ornamented edge; $4\frac{1}{10}$ inches long, by $1\frac{1}{8}$ broad; Wt. 2 dwt. 4 gr.; found in the county of Cavan, in same locality as Nos. 78, 79, and 80. See p. 40. No. 77, a narrow plate, possibly used for confining the hair; 9 inches long, and $\frac{3}{10}$ wide; decorated with a funiform pattern, produced by punching from behind. One extremity is encid. 8d by a narrow collar, probably used for fastening it when complete; Wt. 1 dwt. 2 gr. Nos. 78 to 81, four thin gold plates, apparently parts of the same or similar articles. The extremities of the first and last are rounded off. As now placed, the entire article measures $11\frac{1}{2}$ inches, and weighs 8 dwt. 5 gr. No. 82, a highly decorated golden fillet, figured and described at p. 39. No. 83, a gold breast-pin, figured at p. 41. No. 84, another of the same class, also figured and described at p. 41. No. 85, a small circular gold brooch, with pin, $\frac{3}{4}$ inch wide; has this inscription on back of ring: " ✚ JESUS MARIA, H. VI.;" Wt., 22 gr. No. 86, ditto, somewhat larger; $1\frac{1}{8}$ inch across; Wt., 5 dwt. 3 gr.; on the reverse is the following inscription: "+ PAR + AMVR + FIN + SVI . DVNG." No. 87, a small ring-brooch, ending in a pair of praying hands, with a dagger-like pin; one of a pair; has an inscription round the inner margin, not now sufficiently distinct for transcription; Wt., 1 dwt. 5 gr. No. 88, another of the same size, but somewhat lighter, and differently ornamented; Wt., 22 gr.

No. 89, a contorted armilla, plain; Wt., 7 dwt. 14 gr. Found, along with the bronze celt, No. 578 (Dawson). See p. 430, Vol. I. No. 90, a plain gold penannular armilla, slightly bulbous at extremities; $2\frac{3}{4}$ inches in diameter; Wt., 19 dwt. 16 gr. Found in the county of Carlow, with Nos. 171, 172, 273, and 279. Nos. 91 and 92, two small gold armillæ, each $2\frac{1}{2}$ inches in diameter; the first weighs 6 dwt. 14 gr., and the second 6 dwt. They are both plain, but slightly enlarged at the extremities, and formed a part of the great Clare Find, described at p. 31, and were—*Presented by Charles*

CLASS V.—METALLIC MATERIALS: GOLD—ARMILLÆ. 45

Haliday, Esq. No. 93, a gold armilla, plain, slightly enlarged at extremities; 2¾ inches in diameter; Wt., 1 oz. 7 gr. (Dawson). No. 94, ditto, smaller, plain, oval; 2½ inches in diameter; Wt., 16 dwt. 17 gr. Found, with Nos. 95, 96, 98, and 99, at Strokestown, county of Roscommon, and—*Presented by the Earl of Clarendon.* See p. 51. No. 95, a flat, plain, armilla, apparently unfinished, narrow at extremities; ½ an inch broad; 3 inches wide; Wt., 1 oz. 11 dwt. 13 gr. No. 96, ditto, smaller; Wt., 1 oz. 8 dwt. 12 gr. Found, and presented as above. No. 97, a flat, oval bracelet, figured and described at p. 52 (Sirr). No. 98, ditto, also figured and described at p. 52. No. 99, ditto, 2¾ inches in diameter; extremities broad; Wt., 1 oz. 1 dwt. 6 gr. Found and presented as Nos. 94, 95, 96, and 98.

BRACELETS and ARMILLÆ—in Irish, *Failge Oir*—are of two kinds; Perfect Rings, either plain or twisted, of rare occurrence; and penannular or Unclosed Rings, for apparently a like use, and found in great abundance.* These latter are described in the next section, page 49. The former are well represented by the two following illustrations, drawn one-half the actual size.

Figure 573, No. 27, in Case C, is' from a massive plain ring, 4¼ inches in diameter, on which another small ring plays, like the bronze article figured and described at page

---

* A.D. 3872. "It was Muineamhon that first caused chains of gold [to be worn] on the necks of kings and chieftains in Ireland." Ann. Four Masters; see also Annals of Clonmacnoise, in which it is said he "devised gould to be wrought in chains fit to be worn about men's necks, and rings to be put on their fingers."

A.M. 3882. King Faildeargdoid derived his name from the circumstance of the reddish golden rings then worn upon the hands of the Irish chieftains. Annals of Four Masters, and Annals of Clonmacnoise; see also Keating's History.

A.D. 1150. When Bishop O'Brolchain made the visitation of Cinel-Eoghaine he obtained, among other tributes, "*a gold ring of five ounces*" from Muircheartach O'Loghloinn.

A.D. 1151. When Archbishop Gillamaclaig made the visitation of Connaught, O'Conor gave him "*a ring of gold of 20 ounces;* and O'Brolchain, Bishop of Derry, got a *ring of gold of two ounces weight*, besides a horse and battle-dress, &c., from O'Lyn, Chieftain of Sil-Cathasaigh in Antrim. Annals of the Four Masters, Dr. O'Donovan's Translation.

570, Vol. I. It weighs 11 oz. 14 dwt. 19 gr., and formed a portion of the "Clare Find," described at page 31. Similar articles are occasionally observed sculptured upon the breasts of the statues of ancient Roman generals, the small ring being attached to the dress.*

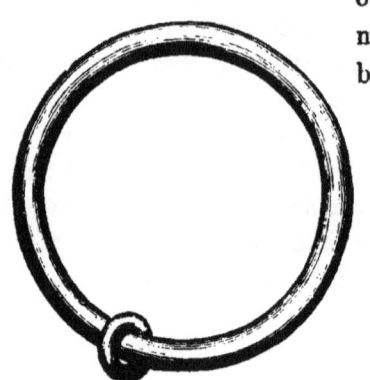

Fig. 573. No. 27.   Fig. 574. No. 193

Figure 574, from No. 193, in Case E, presents us with the finest specimen of the close twisted ring yet discovered in the British Isles. It is 4 inches in the long diameter, weighs 13 oz. 1 dwt. 1 gr., and consists of three rods of gold, each varying in thickness from the size of a man's little finger in the centre, to that of a piece of whipcord at the extremities. These rods are wreathed or twisted together, their outer ends being wrapt round the joining, as shown in the cut, and the other extremities hidden within the coil. It was found in the county of Carlow.

During the period of the Danish invasions, and the partial rule held by that people in certain parts of Ireland, our annals and histories record many plunderings by the Northmen, in which large quantities of gold were carried off. But, with the exception of some iron swords, spears, and a few other

---

* Under the year 876, the Saxon Chronicle informs us that the Danes gave hostages to King Alfred, "and then they swore oaths to him on the holy ring, which they never before would do to any nation;" possibly it may have been on such a ring as that figured above. See also Proc. R. I. A., vol. xii., p. 504.

CLASS V.—METALLIC MATERIALS: GOLD—ARMILLÆ. 47

implements of war, chiefly found in the city of Dublin and its immediate neighbourhood, we have not yet met with any antiquities which would appear to have belonged to that people. Neither do the Collections of Denmark, Norway, or Sweden, except in very few instances, contain any articles that can with certainty be termed Irish. If our gold was carried by the northern invaders to their own country (where they had no native gold of their own), it was probably re-melted for the purposes of Scandinavian jewellery. The gold ornament in the Museum of the Academy, which more particularly bears the impress of Scandinavian art, is the large ring, probably an armlet, figured below, one-half the true size, and

Fig. 575.   No. 290.

which was recently found, it is said, near Clonmacnoise, in the King's County, along with the twisted neck-torque, No. 291, figured at page 74, both now attached to Case E. This consists of a large, thin, hollow ring, 5½ inches in diameter, with a hollow, decorated bulb on one side, and on the other a spiral enlargement, each with an embossed pattern, differing altogether from the style of ornament observed in any of our golden ornaments of native origin, as may be seen by the accompanying cuts, Figs. 576 and 577, both drawn the actual size.

The first represents the large bulbous ornament, in which the enrichment is in relief, and the concave portions between the central and the lateral decorations are punched all over, so as to give them a frosted appearance. All the parts of this ornament are complete and continuous; but in the upper member

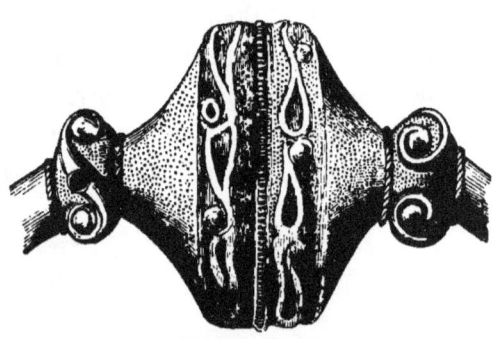

Fig. 576, No. 290.

there is an aperture for a pin or rivet, which fastened the hollow end of the ring at this place. Whether this mode of joining was temporary, it would not be possible, in the present state of the article, to decide.

Fig. 577 shows the enlargement on the opposite side of the ring, and represents a continuous band, which interlaces with itself, and forms a sort of whip-handle-work decoration at this part. Its surface is covered with an involuted raised and embossed pattern, as if made by a

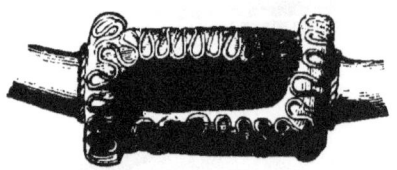

Fig. 577. No. 290.

thread of gold-wire laid upon its surface. The whole article weighs 3 oz. 11 dwt. 12 gr. Similar articles, both in gold and bronze, but wanting the second enlargement, are preserved in the Copenhagen Museum.* The Academy is in-

---

* See Worsaae's *Nordiske Oldsager*, 1859, Plate 56, Fig. 260, and Plate 85 Fig. 367.

debted to the Government for this article, which, together with the neck-torque, No. 291, were the first golden antiquities procured under the recent treasure-trove regulations. Both Pococke and Vallancey have figured and described massive and highly decorated bracelets found in Ireland in their times; the latter mentions the circumstance of "ten golden bracelets," found in Connaught in 1802, having been purchased for £700.*

UNCLOSED RINGS, ARMILLÆ, BRACELETS, and CUP-TERMINATED FIBULÆ, of different shapes, patterns, and styles of ornament, but all bearing a certain amount of affinity to an original type, have been discovered in great quantity, at different times, in Ireland. They have been found either singly or in hoards, as in the great gold find of Clare; and in some instances were crushed together, as if hidden in haste. The frequent mention in our early histories of royal personages having bestowed rings of gold on poets, bards, philosophers, and warriors, and the number of cases in which tribute was paid in similar ornaments, is confirmed by the many instances in which such articles are found throughout the country in the present day.

In addition to the many references given in the foregoing text and notes, we may mention the following. It is related that, in the early part of the first century, the wife of Nuadha Necht, the Poet-King of Leinster, who gave her name of Boann to the River Boyne, used to have her arms covered with rings of gold, for bestowal on poets and men of learning.† This royal patronage of poetry and history affords

---

* The Martyrology of Donegal on 17th June, noticing St. Moling, says, "One night that Moling sent his fishermen to catch fish, they caught a large salmon in the nets; and when it was split open, there was found a ring of gold [*Failge oir*] in its belly, and Moling divided the gold into three parts; one-third he gave to the poor, and one-third to cover a relic, and the other third to do labours and works, &c." A.D. 696.

† See MS. Brehon Law, in Library, Trinity College, Dublin, II. 18, p. 545, quoted in Dr. Petrie's work on the Ecclesiastical Architecture and Round Towers of Ireland, p. 213.

one of many reasons to account for the amount and state of preservation of our domestic annals.

We do not find reference to Anklets,—such objects of personal decoration being chiefly confined to the inhabitants of warm climates, by whom the lower limbs are generally less covered than among people inhabiting the colder regions of the north and west.

The simplest form of bracelet is that of a plain ring, round or oval in shape, about $2\frac{3}{4}$ inches in diameter, to fit the wrist, and either flat or circular in section, unclosed at one side, and having the ends separated for about an inch, for greater facility of adjustment. In most instances, the extremities of the latter are enlarged or dilated into conical bulbs, with flat cymbal-shaped faces; or hollowed into cups, varying from slight, shallow, saucer-like concavities, to those resembling a goblet or the calix of a flower. Most of these rings are thick in the centre, and fine off gradually towards their bulbous ends. Others of a rarer description consist of a square bar of gold, twisted into the torque pattern, but without terminal enlargements. Several of each kind have been found in pairs. It is not unlikely that several bracelets of different patterns were worn together, as in the present day. Some of the plain, flat, and cylindrical rings are arranged in Case C, but the great majority of these specimens of ancient jewellery are in Case D, in the western ground-floor of the Museum. Each variety is illustrated in the following pages.

Golden *Ingots*, generally of an elongated oval form, triangular in section, and of various weights, have from time to time been found in different parts of Ireland; but, as they did not possess artistic value, they have been generally melted. We have one small article of this description in the Academy's Museum, No. 283, in Case F, figured, the natural size, on the opposite page. It weighs 12 dwt. 9 gr. Two similar ingots, the one weighing 3 oz. 12 dwt. 5 gr., and the other 1 oz. 6 dwt. 12 gr., were among the articles discovered at

Mooghaun, county of Clare, already referred to. Each of these ingots could, by a little hammering and manipulation, be turned into a penannular armlet, either flat or cylindrical, and their weights correspond within a few grains with those of some of the armillæ alluded to at p. 31.

Fig. 578. No. 283.

By the two subjoined cuts are shown what would appear to have been stages in the formative process of these armbands. Figure 579 is drawn, the natural size, from a portion of a plain bar of gold, with a bulbous hammered

Fig. 579. No. 284.

end, apparently intended for the usual terminal enlargement of such an article. It is 7½ inches long, and weighs 1 oz. 17 dwt. 6 gr. It was found near Carrigaholt, county of Clare. Figure 580, No. 280, represents a straight bar of wrought gold, thick in the middle, and slightly enlarged at

Fig. 580. No. 280.

the extremities. It is much more finished than the former, measures 6¾ inches in length, and weighs 2 oz. 17 dwt. 1 gr. It is, in fact, finished in all respects, except the curvature, and closely resembles No. 113, in Case **D**. These three articles are attached to Case **F**, and they show that the manufacture of such articles was carried on in this country.

There are five examples of the plain, flat, unclosed hoop of gold in the bottom row of Case **C**, numbered from 95 to 99. In shape and workmanship they greatly resemble similar antique articles in silver found in Ireland. Of the two figured below, No. 98, which is perfectly plain, with slightly everted edges, and somewhat oval in form, measures 2½ inches in diameter, and weighs 1 oz. 4 dwt. 18 gr. It was found, with four others, " lying just between the gravel and turf, at a depth of six feet under the surface, in the townland of Vesnoy, near the ruins of Urney Church," in making a new cut through the demesne of Strokestown, during the arterial drainage operations in the county Roscommon, in 1849, and was—*Presented by the Earl of Clarendon,* then Lord Lieutenant of Ireland.

Fig. 581. No. 98.

Fig. 582. No. 97.

See Proceedings, vol. iv., page 389, and vol. v., page 49, App. No. 97 is slightly decorated, and the hoop contracted towards the ends. It measures 2¼ inches across; weighs 16 dwt. 16 gr.; it was found at Abbey Fore, county of Westmeath, and was procured with the Sirr Collection.

Figure 583, drawn, half size, from No. 191, in Case E, represents a solid armlet, punched all over, like some of the or-

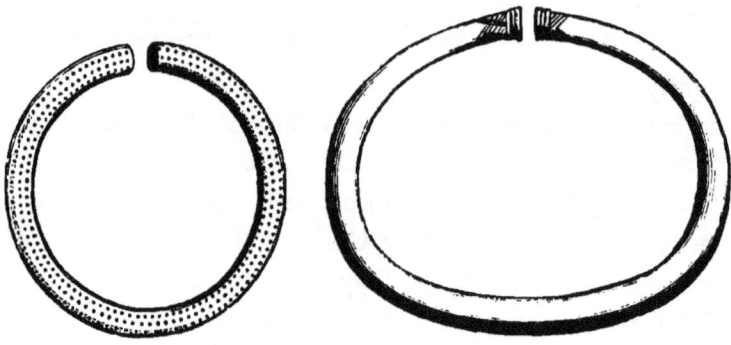
Fig. 583. No. 191.   Fig. 584. No. 194.

namentation on Scandinavian rings. It weighs 2 oz. 1 dwt. 5 gr., and was found, along with a plain but massive gold ring, 12 ounces weight, in the year 1833, near Trimleston Castle, on the Boyne, county of Meath, and was procured with the Dawson Collection.* One of the most beautiful penannular

---

* There is a model of the large ring alluded to above now in the illustrative Collection of the Academy.
See Dublin Penny Journal, vol. i., p. 413, where both rings are delineated

CLASS V.—METALLIC MATERIALS: GOLD—ARMILLÆ. 53

armlets in the Collection is the smooth, massive, cylindrical ring, with ornamented ends, No. 194, in Case **E**, figured above, one-half size. It weighs 3 oz. 15 dwt. 4 gr. See Proceedings, vol. v., p. 85.

The two following cuts, half the size of the originals, illustrate the light torque-shaped armlet, and that with enlarged and slightly cupped extremities, No. 172, in Case **E**, and

Fig. 585. No. 172.　　　　Fig. 586. No. 118.

No. 118, in Case **D**. The former is from a light, four-sided bar of gold, twisted into the torque pattern, and weighing 13 dwt. 17 gr. It was found, with its fellow, No. 171, and other specimens of antique gold manufacture, in the county of Carlow. Similar arm-rings may be seen in the Copenhagen Museum. The latter, No. 118, in Case **D**, is a good specimen of the unclosed bracelet, and differs slightly from the generality of these articles in not being cylindrical, but presenting a flattened quadrangular figure in section. It has the appearance of having been much worn, and its extremities are slightly cupped. It is 3 inches in diameter, weighs 3 oz. 12 dwt. 2 gr., and formed part of the "Clare Find," described

and described by Dr. Petrie. Even so enlightened and philosophical an antiquary as the learned author of that notice, then believed that "rings of this kind were not only used as ornaments, but, before the introduction of minted coin, served as money;" and observed that even the torques and collars "served in lieu of money." That such valuables may have been occasionally used in barter, and, in the same way as cattle or any other marketable commodity, passed from hand to hand in these early times, before the introduction of coin, cannot be denied; but that they were originally intended for such purposes, or bore any specific value beyond that of gold, or that they were made any particular weight, remains to be proved.

at page 31. Similar penannular articles of bronze, with enlarged extremities, are occasionally found in Ireland, of which Fig. 479, page 570, Vol. I., is a good example. There are nineteen armillæ arranged at top of Case **D**, the details of which are given at page 66.

As may be seen by a careful inspection of the specimens of nearly every variety of weapon, tool, or ornament in our Collection, a gradual process of development of some particular part, or of some special design or style of decoration, is carried on throughout a series of articles, not always applied to the same purpose, but traceable from the rudest to the most elaborate examples of ancient art. This principle is very apparent in the transition from the simple unclosed ring, evidently used as an armlet, to a wide-spread fibula, with broad, shallow, or saucer-shaped extremities, as shown in the following section, under the head of Mammillary Brooches, and as a glance at Case **D** affords convincing proof. First, we have the plain cylindrical ring, enlarged at the ends into flat, button-shaped knobs, as in Nos. 100 to 104, 106, 113, 115, and 116. Then the ends become slightly concave, as shown by Nos. 105, 107 to 112, 114, 117, and 118; afterwards they were deepened into cup or goblet-shaped terminations, many of which are adorned round their lips, and where the collars join the stems, with the usual lineal engraving, so characteristic of early Irish art. At the same time, the hoop was made either hollow or semicircular in section, as if to economise the material; for examples of which, see Nos. 141 to 145, and 148 and 150. Finally, the ring or hoop was lessened in girth, and spread outwards, and the dish-shaped terminations enlarged and expanded, until it is manifest that the article was applied to another purpose, and became a fastener, and not a bracelet, as may be seen in Nos. 120 and 121. But the transition is so gradual, even in the comparatively limited number of specimens presented by the Academy's Collection, that it is difficult to decide where the armilla ends and the brooch or fibula commences.* The same change by which one part of an article is retrenched, and another enlarged and developed, so as to become the chief object of decoration or of use, is well seen in the ring-brooches of bronze and silver.' The following engravings illustrate this position. Figure 587, drawn from No. 111, represents, half size, a cylindrical unclosed ring, weighing 1 oz. 8 dwt. 22 gr., with thin, hollow, goblet-shaped extremities, half an inch deep, decorated round their edges by raised fillets, and having slightly engraved circular and zig-zag lines round the hoop for about an inch below their

Fig. 587. No. 111.   Fig. 588. No. 142.

attachments. In Figure 588, also drawn, half-size, from No. 142, may be seen the same variety of article on a larger scale, in which the handle is hollow, and the flower-shaped cups are beautifully engraved both within and without their lips. The collars are also decorated with the dog-tooth form of ornament, which, however, only occupies two-thirds of the circle,—probably to economize labour. Presuming that this article was worn on the wrist, we can only account for the retention of the cups by supposing that it was the fashion or style of art of

* This shows the necessity for the guardians of a public collection obtaining and arranging in their proper places every article which *can* be procured, so that as many links as possible in the chain of art may be exhibited together. Possibly these different varieties in form and style of decoration, among our antique gold ornaments, may have indicated different grades in society;—but on this subject nothing is yet certain.

the period, a reason equally applicable to many unaccountable fashions in the jewellery of the present day. It weighs 2 oz. 4 dwt. 5 gr., and was found in the townland of Faunrusk, parish of Templemaley, near Ballyvaughan, county of Clare, in 1859.

In Figure 589, drawn, half-size, from No. 139, the hoop is very slender, and the cups deep and conical, with filleted edges. It weighs 17 dwt. 13 gr. In No. 150, the last article at the bottom of Case **D**, represented below, one-third the true size, by figure 590, the cups are shallow, and the hoop semilunar in section. It weighs 4 oz. 7 dwt. 1 gr. These articles were both procured with the Dawson Collection.

Fig. 589. No. 139.

Hundreds of those unclosed hoops, with terminal cups, have been found in Ireland, and specimens of them may be seen in most of our Museums. The celebrated full-sized bas-relief of the Roman standard-bearer, not long since discovered in the vicinity of Mayence, throws much light upon several of our ancient ornaments. The right fore-arm is decorated with unclosed armillæ; two penannular fibulæ, with enlarged and decorated terminations, are suspended from a strap which passes across the breast, and beneath these there are rows of circular *phaleræ*, like the round gold plates which will be found figured and described at page 83. Both these ornaments are regarded by Lindenschmit* and other German antiquaries as decorations analogous to the medals worn in modern times. Presuming that certain ranks, professions, or grades of society in Ireland wore particular forms of ring or fibula decoration, we have at once a clue to the

Fig. 590. No. 150.

---

* " *Die Altherthümer unserer heidinschen Vorzeit,*" Heft iv., Tafel 6.

varieties and form of ornamentation to be seen even in those gold articles which have been preserved to the present day.

There are at present forty-six golden armillæ in the Academy's Collection, 11 in Case **C**, 27 in **D**, 5 in **E**, and 3 in **F**.

MAMMILLARY FIBULÆ.—For the sake of distinction and arrangement, we have applied this term to a class of gold ornaments, of great diversity of size, found in abundance in Ireland. They have been attached to Case **D**, in the Western Compartment of the ground-floor of the Museum, adjoining the door of the Moore Library.

As we traced the gradual formation of the cup from the flattened knob, as described in the foregoing section, so we may here follow the further development of that part to its greatest extent, among articles in which the staple-shaped handle portion becomes of secondary importance. Intermediate between these two varieties, represented by Figs. 588 and 592, there is another, in which the handle is wider, proportionably thinner, and less annular; and in which the discs are broader, shallower, and not attached by their centres, but towards their inner margins. Nos. 120 and 121, in Case **D**, are good examples of this variety. The former is here represented, one-half the actual size, and is further

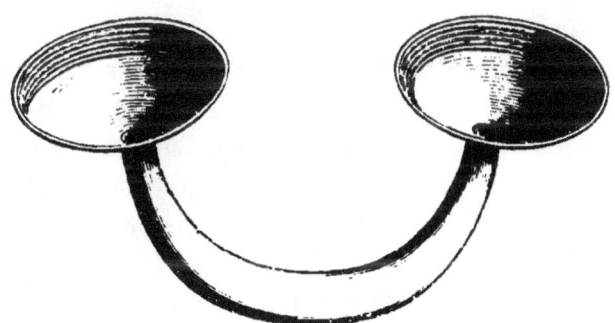

Fig. 591. No. 120.

remarkable for having the apertures between the shallow, saucer-shaped discs and the hollow handle still unclosed. It was probably left unfinished at that part. It is the second largest fibula in the Collection, is of bright yellow gold, and in fine preservation. The edges of the cups are decorated with thorough flutings, one of the few instances of that peculiarity in this variety of ornament in the Museum. Each cup is 2¼ inches in diameter; and when the article is laid on the flat of these portions, it stands 2½ inches high. It weighs 5 oz. 5 dwt. 16 gr.* There are eight articles of this description at present in the Collection, Nos. 120 to 122, and 146 to 150. This last No., however already figured at p. 56, partakes more of the character of an armilla than a fibula.

The subjoined engraving, Figure 592, drawn, one-third size, from No. 122, represents the largest example of the mam-

Fig. 592. No. 122.

millary fibula which is known to have remained to the present day. It consists of two broad, cup-shaped discs, each 5 inches in diameter, set 1¾ inch apart, and united by a staple like the handle of a drawer, as seen in the foregoing illustration. The entire article measures 11 inches in length, and weighs 16 oz. 17 dwt. 4 gr. The internal surfaces of the cups bear marks of hammering all over them. The comparatively short, thick handle is hollow, and measures 4⅛ inches in circumference at

---

* Mr. Law, of Sackville-street, possesses a very fine specimen of gold fibula, in shape somewhat between that of the foregoing and Fig. 590. The handle portion is lozenge-shaped in section. It weighs 6 oz. It has been in his establishment for many years.

the broadest part. Placed on the flat, it stands 3⅜ inches high. The edges of the cups are turned over, and decorated externally with deeply-grooved flutings; and a smaller, but similar form of ornament encircles each neck, or narrow portion of the handle. Each cup, which is 1⅝ inch deep, gradually slopes inwards from without, for about 4¼ inches, to the point of junction with the handles, which would appear to have been attached after they were made. This beautiful article was found in the year 1819, at Castlekelly, county of Roscommon, five feet deep in gravel, below where fifteen " spit" of turf had been cut, and it was for a long time believed to be brass. It was procured by D. H. Kelly, Esq., for the late Dean Dawson, and came into the Museum with that gentleman's Collection.

Various have been the conjectures respecting the uses of gold ornaments of this description; but an examination of kindred articles in bronze, preserved in the Museums of Copenhagen and Mayence, sets the question at rest. They were fibulæ, or brooches, in the fastening of which a portion of the soft woollen cloak or mantle passed in between the cups or discs, into the space under the handle, and was there fastened by means of an *acus* or pin, temporarily affixed to one side of the handle, where it joins the cup. In some instances, the ends of the pin were bifid, and clasped round the handle by means of a spring, as in the case of a bronze fibula in the Copenhagen Museum, figured by Worsaae, in the last edition of his *Nordiske Oldsager.* See Plate 51, Fig. 231. In other instances, as those in the Mayence Museum, of one of which there is a model in the Academy's Comparative Collection, the pin was fixed by means of an unclosed ring, attached to one extremity. In wearing, it is very possible that the pin was first passed through the dress, and then adjusted to the brooch by means of its spring, or open ring; but by what other devices these ornaments were held in position, we have now no means of determining. Upon a careful examination of a great number of mammillary fibulæ, we have found two circumstances corroborative of the foregoing observation. The places in which these articles have been most worn are invariably at the junction of the handles with the cups, where the loop or clasp at the extremity of the pin would play; and also the edges of the cups, where they would rub naturally against the person.

In the Museum of Trinity College there is a magnificent fibula of this description, with solid handle and massive cups, which weighs 33 ounces (the heaviest now known to exist), and decorated all over the external surface of the cups with circular indentations surrounding a central indented spot; it has also a very elegantly engraved decoration encircling each collar, where the handle is joined to the cups, the inside lips of which are also beautifully ornamented. It is 8⅜ inches long. The cups are more bell-shaped than in that belonging to the Academy, Fig. 592, and are also set on to the handle at a different angle, possibly to adjust it to the part of the

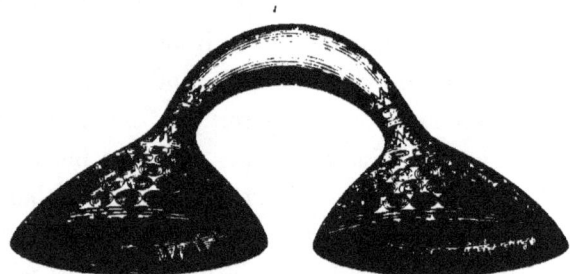

Fig. 593.

shoulder where we know, from some of the Roman and Frankish statues, the ancients occasionally wore the fibula.*

The accompanying illustration, one-third the size of the original, affords a faithful representation of this most beautiful article, which stands nearly 3½ inches high.† Within the last

* See *Die Vaterländischen Alterthümer. der Fürstlich Hohenzoller'schen Sammlungen zu Sigmaringen.* Mainz: 1860. S. 53, Fig. 35.

† See the coloured drawing of this and other Irish antiquities in the College

two years, a remarkably fine article of this description was discovered near Keeper Mountain, county of Tipperary, by some peasants, who sawed it across; and the greater portion of it was shortly afterwards sold to a Dublin jeweller for less than its bullion value, and melted forthwith.* Pococke and Vallancey have figured and described massive articles of this description, several of them beautifully decorated. The latter author, who called them "double-headed pateræ," supposed them to have been used in " libations to the two chief deities of the heathen Irish, viz., Budh and his son Pharamon, and also to the sun and moon !"† The decorations and dog's-tooth ornament on one of these articles he describes as typical representations of the elements, water and fire, and also says—"The twelve circles may have represented the twelve signs of the zodiac, and their spheres. The forty-eight pyramids correspond with the number of the old constellations; and the seven triangles of the handle to that of the planets."—*Collectanea*, vol. vi., p. 240. Such were the interpretations offered and received sixty years ago, by not a few, for the mere artistic decoration of an Irish ornament! The learned Bishop, however, was not so speculative, but says,—"whether it be a species of fibula, or what else, I am utterly at a loss. Many such, diversified by only a few ornaments, have been found, from time to time, in different parts of Ireland."‡ That distinguished antiquary published a drawing of one, found in the county of Galway, which weighed 15 oz. Vallancey has figured a very remarkable one, about 9 inches long, but 4¼ in the widest portion of the bow of the handle, which was found in

Museum, in Table 52, of the Catalogue of Illustrations in the Academy, and also the model of it in the Comparative Collection.

* It is described by the Rev. Jas. Graves in the Proceedings of the Kilkenny Archæological Society—see vol. 2, N. S., p. 445.

† Letter to Rev. J Dubourdieu, in the Statistical Survey of Antrim, published in 1812, p. 585.

‡ Archæologia, vol. ii., p. 40.

the county of Galway, and weighed 52 guineas. Others, mentioned by Simon and Pococke, were also found in that locality.*

One of the largest mammillary fibulæ recorded is that which was engraved by Dr. Dubourdieu, in his *Statistical Survey of the County of Antrim*, in 1812. It was not unlike that now in the Academy, Fig. 592, but was much more highly decorated. It measured 11½ inches in length, and weighed 19 oz. 10 dwt. Vallancey gave casts of two large fibulæ of this description to the Museum of Trinity College. They are very large, plain, and massive, the handles being wider and more arched, and the cups smaller and deeper than in any of the before-mentioned. One of these would appear to have been made from that represented by No. 2, pl. vi., vol. iv., of the *Collectanea*, which weighed 10 oz.

In the illustrative Collection of the Academy, there is a metal cast, presented by Dr. Petrie, of a very remarkable article of this description. The handle is large, massive, deeply bowed, embraced by a collar in the centre, and gradually enlarges into small, shallow, cup-shaped extremities. It stands 3¾ inches high, and is 7¼ in length. The original, which weighed 40 oz. 10 dwt., was discovered many years ago on the estate of the late Henry Adair, Esq., near Dunboyne, in the county of Meath.

In the lower portion of Case **D**, have been arranged a number of kindred articles, but proportionally wider, and more slender in the handles, and having smaller cups. In most of these the handles are hollow, as in No. 142, Fig. 588.

---

* Mr. Simon's unpublished paper, referred to by Pococke in the Archæologia, vol. ii., has at length been discovered in the Archives of the Society of Antiquaries of London; and I am indebted to the courtesy of its present Secretary, Mr. C. K. Watson, for a copy of it. In one of the fibulæ described and figured by Simon, and which was about the size of No. 120 in the Academy's Collection (see Fig. 591, p. 57), the handle is beautifully decorated over its entire length. It is that figured by Pococke in the Archæologia, vol. ii., plate iii., fig. 1.

CLASS V.—METALLIC MATERIALS: GOLD—FIBULÆ. 63

The subjoined illustration represents another variety of the same class of ornament, but differing from the former in having the discs perfectly flat, thin, and plain, and the solid connecting bow or handle invariably highly decorated with longitudinal groovings. This specimen, No. 123, is 5 inches in length, and each circular plate 2¾ in diameter. Upon the external face of one of the plates is a small loop, possibly for the purpose of attaching a pin or a string to. This fact

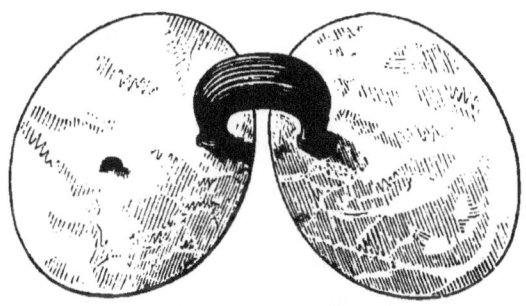

Fig. 594. No. 123.

strengthens the conjecture already expressed, as to the object and use of these articles. It weighs 4 oz. 15 dwt. 19 gr., and was procured with the Dawson Collection.*

Below the centre of Case **D** have been arranged fourteen articles of this description, varying in size from that of the foregoing, to No. 124, Fig. 597, which is but half an inch in diameter, and weighs only 2 dwt. 8 gr. In this descending scale, the plates gradually lessen until they disappear altogether, as shown in the an-

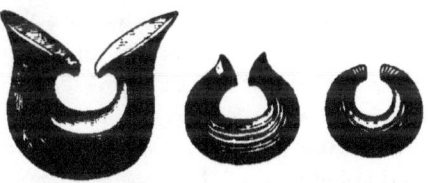

Fig. 595. No. 133. Fig. 596. No. 125. Fig. 597. No. 124.

---

* A similar gold article, with a small loop on the external face of one of the thin circular plates, has been figured by Vallancey in the *Collectanea*, vol. iv., Pl. xiv., Fig. 7, and described as an *Aisin*, which was "suspended by a string round the neck, and hung at the breast. On the external plate is a small loop, into which was fixed a slender golden wire, on which perched the Augur's favourite bird: the Hibernian Druids fixed on the wren!"—p. 96.

nexed illustration, representing, the true size, Nos. 133, 125, and 124. The grooving upon these snail-shaped articles has been effected with great precision, and adds a special lustre to the metal. The extremity of each is also beautifully tooled, apparently by engraving, as may be seen in the foregoing illustrations; but in every instance the inner curvature is plain. In No. 133, weighing 17 dwt. 7 gr., the terminal enlargements are turned slightly into the hollow of the bow; it was—*Presented by J. H. Monck Mason, Esq.* See Proceedings, vol. ii., page 272. No. 125 weighs 7 dwt. 12 gr., and has the ends slightly enlarged, as if for the purpose of attachment of plates, like those in Fig. 594. Figure 596, No. 125, was procured with the Dawson Collection. In No. 124, Fig. 597, there are no enlargements whatever; it is the second least specimen in the Collection; while No. 137, on the opposite side of the semicircle in which these articles are arranged on Case D, is less in size, but weighs 9 grains more. All these articles were at one time supposed to be "ring money;" but an examination of the weights of this series will show the absurdity of this theory.*

* Sir William Betham carried his "ring money" theory so far as to assert that not only these, but every unclosed ring of any metal,—gold, silver, bronze, or iron, plain or decorated, square, flat, twisted, or cylindrical, with or without cups, plates, or expanded extremities, and from the weight of 48 grains to 36 ounces,—was a specimen of "money." In his *Etruria Celtica*, vol. ii. p. iii., he copied (but without the slightest acknowledgment) Mr. Dubourdieu's plate of the large Antrim fibula, already referred to at p. 61, as an illustration of his views. He also says, "It was found in a stone chest." Now, none of our gold antiquities have been found in stone chests,—the small sepulchral *Kistvaens* of the early Irish,—nor in caverns referable to a very remote period, but almost invariably in the ground, in bog or upland. In General Vallancey's letter to the Rev. G. Dubourdieu, published in 1812—the only record of that "find"—it is stated that it was "sold by a peasant, who said he dug it up in the parish of Ballymoney."—See note, p. 61, of this Catalogue. Further, to show the inaccuracy of that writer, it may be mentioned that the weight of the Ballymoney fibula was 19 oz. 10 dwt., and not 19 oz., as mentioned in the *Etruria Celtica*. Again, Sir William Betham says in the same place—"Vallancey mentions one which weighed 56 oz." Two others are mentioned by Vallancey—"one 15 oz. and the other 1 oz. 12 grs." The author of the *Collectanea* nowhere mentions a

It is quite possible that the small crescentic articles, without plates, like No. 125, Fig. 596, are unfinished; for it is manifest that the discs might have been attached after the handle portions were completed, and perhaps engraved.

The following may have been the method by which these articles, both large and small, were employed as studs or fasteners between the button-holes of the dress. The accompanying figure, drawn in perspective the exact size, from the

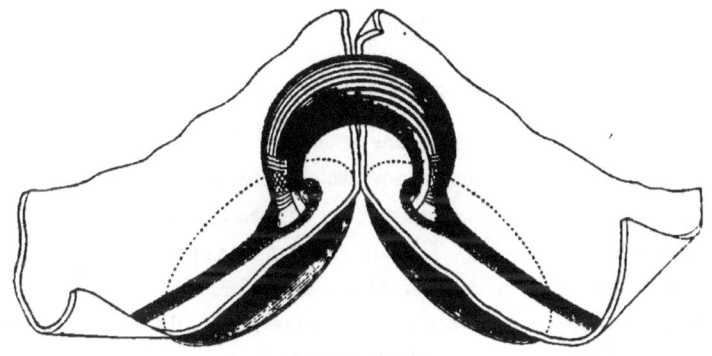

Fig. 598. No. 130.

fibula, No. 130 (which weighs 1 oz. 5 dwt.), also represents a fragment of dress, through the slits in which the plates were passed,—the portions of texture between the apertures occupying the space beneath the decorated hoop. We have experimentally assured ourselves of the feasibility of this process. A row of such studs, either of equal size, or decreasing gradually from one end to the other, would form a very beautiful decoration to the vest or tunic. The thin, perfectly plain, circular plates would, in all probability, have been engraved,

---

fibula of 56 oz., but in Vol. vi., p. 237, plate xiii., describes one (already alluded to in the text) as having been sold in Dublin "for fifty-two guineas, its weight." The one "weighing 15 oz." was not known to Vallancey, but he quotes Bishop Pococke's description of it, on the page facing his plate of the Galway fibula, and this may have led to Sir W. Betham's mistake. These errors, out of many which might be recorded, show the general looseness and inaccuracy of that author's statements in his Essay on "Ring Money."

or otherwise decorated, had they been intended for show, and not utility. In the specimen from which the foregoing illustration was made, the junction of these plates with the expanded ends of the bow is still manifest. It is also possible that some of the larger fibulæ and mammillary brooches may have been adjusted to the cloak or mantle in somewhat the same way as that described above, either by means of loops or button-holes.*

The following list gives the details of the various fibulæ not described in the foregoing section:—

WESTERN GROUND FLOOR.

Case **D** contains seventy-one articles of the species denominated fibulæ, armillæ, and ring-money, &c., chiefly consisting of ununited rings, with either plain, enlarged, or cupped extremities; and numbered from 100 to 170. The top row consists of a number of rings open on one side, and apparently used as bracelets or armlets, in which the enlarged extremities increase gradually, from a small, solid bulb, flat on the face, to a thin, conical cup, or goblet-shaped end. No. 100 is a light penannular article, circular in section, with flat terminations, $2\frac{3}{8}$ inches in long diameter; Weight, 7 dwt. 11 gr. No. 101, ditto, a finer specimen, oval; $2\frac{3}{8}$ inches wide; Wt., 8 dwt. 11 gr. No. 102, ditto, very similar; $2\frac{1}{2}$ inches; Wt., 8 dwt. 18 gr.; said to have been procured at Tullow, county of Carlow (Sirr). No. 103, ditto; $2\frac{3}{8}$ inches wide; Wt., 9 dwt. 3 gr. No. 104, ditto, larger; bent irregularly; Wt., 1 oz. 17 gr. No. 105, ditto, flat,

---

* Even Vallancey, with all his absurd fancies, was of opinion that these bows, with "circular flat ends," were fibulæ; that the discs passed through the button-holes, and lay flat on the body, and that the chased or ornamented part was turned forwards; yet he did not see that the *Aisin* referred to in the note at p. 63, and resembling our Fig. 590, was of precisely the same shape, and evidently intended for a similar purpose; and that the identical article had been figured and described by Pococke long previously, with these observations—"It was made use of to fasten a cloak or other loose garment by passing it through an opening worked on each side for this purpose." In matters of fact and illustration, Vallancey's plagiarisms of Pococke are as patent as the adoption without acknowledgment of the General's opinions by more modern writers.

CLASS V.—METALLIC MATERIALS: GOLD—FIBULÆ. 67

four-sided in section, extremities large and somewhat cupped; diameter 2⅜ inches; Wt., 16 dwt. 10 gr. No. 106, a thick penannular ring, with the enlarged extremities flat on the face; 2⅜ inches diameter; Wt., 1 oz. 9 dwt. 20 gr. No. 107, an arm-ring, like No. 105; discs slightly cupped; 2⅝ inches in diameter; Wt., 1 oz. 3 dwt. 5 gr. No. 108, ditto, larger, extremities enlarged and slightly dished; diameter 2¾ inches; Wt., 1 oz. 11 dwt. 17 gr. No. 109, a penannular armlet, with large cup-shaped extremities; diameter 2½ inches: Wt., 1 oz. 1 gr. No. 110, ditto, circular in bar, fining off towards the ends, extremities cup-shaped; 2½ inches in diameter; Wt., 11 dwt. 19 gr. No. 111, ditto, figured and described at p. 55. No. 112, ditto, not so massive, extremities saucer-shaped; diameter 2⅝ inches; 1¼ between inner edges of discs; Wt., 1 oz. 2 dwt. 7 gr. No. 113, a penannular arm-ring, large, massive, bar circular, extremities slightly expanded and flattened; diameter 3⅛ inches; Wt., 2 oz. 9 dwt. No. 114, ditto, light, extremities cup-shaped; 2⅜ inches in diameter; Wt., 19 dwt. 11 gr.; stated by Mr. Clibborn, in the Official Catalogue of the Dublin Exhibition of 1853, to have been found in the cinerary box, No. 275, in Case F. No. 115, ditto; 2½ inches in diameter; ends flat; Wt., 1 oz. 2 gr.; said to have been found in box, No. 277, Case F. No. 116, a massive oval ring, circular in section, extremities unclosed and slightly enlarged; 3 inches in diameter; Wt., 4 oz. 11 dwt. 3 gr. No. 117, a massive armlet, with slightly cupped extremities; diameter 3½ inches; Wt., 4 oz. 3 dwt. 2 gr.; part of the "Clare Find." No. 118, ditto, on opposite side of Tray; figured and described at p. 53. No. 119, in centre of circle of "ring-money," the broken-off cup of a large fibula, decorated round the margin with three grooved lines, which pass through the substance of the metal, like No. 120; oval; the apex of the cone to one side of centre, where there are the remains of the double plate by which this portion was attached to the handle; 2⅞ inches by 2¾; Wt., 1 oz. 11 gr. No. 120, a large fibula, figured and described at p. 57. No. 121, on the opposite side of the Tray, ditto, but smaller, handle apparently solid; decorated on the inside margins of cups with three elevated lines, but perfectly plain on the outside; total length 5¼ inches; stands 2¼ high; each cup is 2⅛ wide; Wt., 4 oz. 11 dwt. 2 gr.—*Presented by the Marquis of Kil-*

F 2

dare. See Proc., Vol. iii., p. 138. No. 122, the largest fibula in the Collection, placed in centre of Case, figured and described at p. 58.

No. 123, the large flat-plated fibula, figured and described at p. 63. In a semicircle beneath it have been arranged fourteen similar articles of smaller size, in which the terminal plates are flat, and gradually developed until they reach their maximum in No. 130. No. 124, a small, solid, penannular ring, with deeply-grooved ornament on its convexity, no plates, figured at p. 63. No. 125, ditto, larger. See Fig. 596, p. 63. No. 126, ditto, plates become developed, tooling on handle sharper and more regular than in foregoing; length $\frac{3}{4}$ inch; Wt., 7 dwt. 11 gr. No. 127, ditto, larger, plates still more developed; the collar spreads out into the plate on each side, unlike No. 123, in which it would appear that the plates were superadded; length $\frac{7}{8}$ inch; Wt., 10 dwt. 12 gr. No. 128, ditto, about the same size; plates somewhat larger, measuring $\frac{9}{8}$ inch in diameter; Wt., 11 dwt. 22 gr. No. 129, ditto, still larger and heavier, decoration and plates the same; Wt., 13 dwt. 20 gr. No. 130, the largest of these small fibulæ, is $1\frac{1}{4}$ inch long, each circular plate $1\frac{1}{8}$ wide, collars of connecting loop highly decorated; Wt., 1 oz. 5 dwt. No. 131, ditto, heavier in hoop, but smaller in plates; $1\frac{3}{8}$ inch long; each plate 1 wide; Wt., 1 oz. 7 dwt. 7 gr. No. 132, ditto, smaller, plates battered; $1\frac{1}{4}$ inch in diameter; Wt., 13 dwt. 17 gr.; found near Kells (Sirr). No. 133, ditto, figured and described at p. 63. No. 134, ditto, smaller, with slight, thin, terminal enlargements; length, 1 inch; Wt., 8 dwt. 6 gr. No. 135, ditto; Wt., 8 dwt. 7 gr. No. 136, ditto, small, no enlargements; $\frac{9}{8}$ inch in length; Wt., 4 dwt. 7 gr. No. 137, ditto, crescent-shaped; $\frac{1}{2}$ inch in diameter; the smallest specimen in the Collection; Wt., 2 dwt. 17 gr. No. 138, a penannular ring, with very deep wineglass-shaped extremities; 3 inches in diameter; Wt., 2 oz. 6 dwt. 20 gr. No. 139, ditto, figured and described at p. 56. No. 140, ditto, more massive, decorated round edges of cups and collars; Wt., 2 oz. 15 dwt. 17 gr. No. 141, ditto, larger, massive, undecorated, handle hollow, lip of each cup everted; diameter, $2\frac{3}{4}$ inches; Wt., 3 oz. 5 dwt. 22 gr.; found near Castlebar, county of Mayo. No. 142, ditto, figured and described at p. 55. No. 143, ditto, handle hollow, and fractured;

CLASS V.—METALLIC MATERIALS: GOLD—FIBULÆ.   69

cups deep, wide, and decorated round edges; diameter 3¼ inches; Wt., 1 oz. 14 dwt. 12 gr. No. 144, ditto, cups goblet-shaped, with inverted edges; collars decorated with circular bands and dog-tooth ornament, which latter, as in No. 142, is defective internally. Such is the usual form of decoration in all these articles. The margins of the cups are decorated with a lightly engraved chevron pattern; diameter 3¼ inches; Wt., 2 oz. 16 dwt. 5 gr. No. 145, ditto, bent, handle hollow, cups deep, thin; decorated round edges and at neck with herring-bone ornament; diameter 3⅜ inches; Wt., 1 oz. 4 dwt. 8 gr.

The last row contains five fibulæ, wider in the handles than any of the former, and with shallow, saucer-shaped extremities. The handles are solid, and either semi-oval or four-sided. No. 146, wide, massive; handle slender, cups shallow; resembles the large fibula, No.121; 3½ inches across; Wt., 2 oz. 16 dwt. 1 gr.; found in the county of Leitrim. No. 147, ditto, cups thicker, and still more shallow, with everted lips; handle four-sided; 4⅜ inches wide; Wt., 3 oz. 18 dwt. 19 gr. No. 148, ditto, cups broad, deep, with inverted edges, and slightly decorated on inner margins, each 2 inches wide; a section of the handle would be a segment of a circle; diameter 4⅞ inches; Wt., 2 oz. 11 dwt. 7 gr. No. 149, ditto, handle solid; cups thin, wide, and shallow; Wt., 3 oz. 6 dwt. 12 gr. No. 150, ditto, figured and described at p. 56.

In a semicircle around the detached boss, No. 119, above the large fibulæ, are a series of fifteen small unclosed rings, usually denominated "ring-money," described at p. 87; and, below them, a row of five specimens of forgeries of the same class of article. These articles are numbered from 151 to 170, the numbering commencing with a very small ring on the right-hand side of the Case. They increase in size to No. 158, and then decrease to No. 165, on the opposite side. No. 151, a very small unclosed ring, measuring ¾ of an inch wide, figured and described at p. 88. No. 152, ditto, somewhat larger, plain; Wt., 1 dwt. 16 gr. No. 153, ditto, larger; ½ inch in diameter; Wt., 2 dwt. 17 gr. No. 154, ditto, larger and thicker; Wt., 3 dwt. 17 gr. No. 155, ditto, larger, but not quite so thick; Wt., 3 dwt. 12 gr. No. 156, ditto, thick, massive, striped, with the indentations very perceptible; ¾ of an inch wide; Wt., 6 dwt. 7 gr.;

No. 157, an unclosed ring, thick, massive, plain; Wt., 7 dwt. 4 gr. No. 158, the largest ring of the set; $\frac{11}{16}$ of an inch wide; barred; striping narrow and close, much worn externally, but very distinct along inner circle; Wt., 11 dwt. 19 gr. From this number the articles decrease in size to No. 165. No. 159, plain, massive. See Fig. 621, p. 88. No., 160, ditto, smaller, striped. See Fig. 622, p. 88. No. 161, ditto, plain, smaller, of reddish gold, like that in fashion some years ago; Wt., 2 dwt. 11 gr. No. 162, ditto, smaller, narrow towards extremities; yellow gold; Wt., 2 dwt. 6 gr. No. 163, ditto, not so thick; Wt., 1 dwt. 16 gr. No. 164, a remarkable form, thick in the middle, and tapering towards the ends, like the snail-shaped handles of the flat-plated fibulæ; Wt., 2 dwt. 13 gr. No. 165, ditto, very diminutive; the least in the Collection; Wt., 14 gr.

Forgeries, consisting of unclosed rings, covered with gold plate, and numbered from 166 to 170, form the bottom row. No. 166, in good preservation, a copper ring, covered with a thin plate of gold, slightly open at top; Wt., 5 dwt. 1 gr. No. 167, ditto, larger, cut across; Wt., 10 dwt. 19 gr. No. 168, ditto, still larger, cut to show the copper centre; Wt., 12 dwt, 6 gr. No. 169, ditto, perfect; Wt., 8 dwt. 14 gr. No. 170, ditto; Wt., 7 dwt. 11 gr.

Of the foregoing articles, Nos. 100, 105, 109, 110, 112, 113, 116, 122, 123, 125, 127, 128, 129, 131, 134 to 139, 143 to 147, 150 to 156, and 159 to 165, were procured with the Dawson Collection.

TORQUE—in Irish, *Torc*—is a term applied to a ring of twisted metal, generally gold, worn either on the neck; round the waist; across the breast; or on the limbs, as an armilla or finger-ring. The simplest form is that of a square bar of gold, twisted so as to present a funicular, or rope-like figure. In the more complex forms, two or more flat strips of metal, joined at their inner edges, are twisted together spirally. The name is expressive of the form.

Decorative articles of this description were known to the Egyptians, the Persians, the people of Persepolis, the Gauls, the early Britons ; and, in later times, to the Romans, on the

CLASS V.—METALLIC MATERIALS: GOLD—TORQUES. 71

coins and monuments of which latter they are figured; but to the Irish Celt they seem to have belonged as a special and frequent form of decoration. They are frequently mentioned in our early Irish histories; and more golden torques have been discovered in this country, and are to be seen in more varieties, and of greater magnitude, in the Museum of the Academy, than in the collections of all the other countries of Europe collectively. They amount to thirty-seven specimens, which, except No. 291, in Case F, have been arranged on Case E. Typical examples of each variety are afforded by the following illustrations. The ends of the torque form loops, which hook into one another, and present great diversity of design and ornamentation.

In the subjoined woodcut have been grouped three varie-

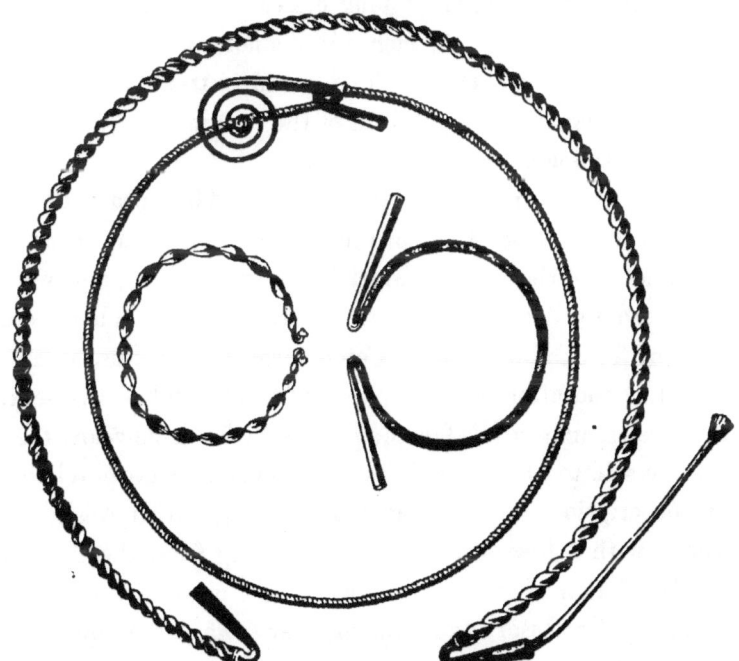

[Fig. 599. No. 192.   Fig. 600. No. 173.   Fig. 601. No. 181.   Fig. 602. No. 174.

ties of torque. The most external, figure 599, from No. 192, is the largest ever known to have been found; it measures

5 feet 7 inches in length, and is 15½ inches in diameter when closed. It is formed of four flat bars of gold, united together at their edges when straight, and then twisted—an artistic process now very difficult to achieve—the whole being $\frac{9}{16}$ths of an inch in diameter. The terminations are prolonged into strong, circular, recurved bars, one of which is drawn out into a projecting arm, 10½ inches in length, and terminates in a short conical knob. It was probably worn obliquely *across the breast*, with the projecting member in front, where it might have served to hang the bridle-rein upon. It weighs 27 oz. 7 dwt. 20 gr., and is the heaviest article of antique manufactured gold now in the Academy's Collection. No. 173, Fig. 600, placed in the illustration immediately within the former, is another torque, lighter and smaller than the foregoing, and having the roping closer. It measures 5 feet 6 inches in length, is 14½ inches in diameter of the ring, and weighs 12 oz. 7 dwt. 13 gr. The coiled extremity is, in all likelihood, not the original form of the terminal bar, which is similar in shape to that of No. 192.

These two magnificent torques were found by a peasant-boy, in 1810, in the side of one of the clay raths at Tara, near the monuments of the Druids, Mael Blocc and Bluicni, and were purchased by Alderman West, of Skinner-row. They were brought for exhibition to St. Petersburgh by the Russian ambassador, and afterwards disposed of to the Duke of Sussex. After remaining in His Grace's possession for some years, they were re-sold to Mr. James West, and, in 1839, were purchased by subscription, and presented to the Royal Irish Academy, where, with a few other articles remaining from the date of the foundation of the institution, and the cross of Cong, presented by Professor Mac Cullagh, they formed the nucleus of the present Collection.*

---

* See Proceedings, vol. i., p. 349. See also the Dublin Penny Journal, vol. i., p. 156, and Dr. Petrie's Essay on the History and Antiquities of Tara Hill, in th

Of the *Waist-Torque*—evidently too large for the neck, and too small to be worn across the breast—we have a good example in No. 179, described at page 79, which, though 44½ inches in length, and 13 in diameter of hoop, weighs only 3 oz. 3 dwt. 15 gr. The ends of this variety are not prolonged, and do not stand out like those of the breast-torques, but terminate in simple hooks. No. 180, described at page 80, is of a like description, but formed of a plain, quadrangular, untwisted bar of gold, with round hooked terminations. It measures 3 feet 1½ inch in length, and weighs 9 oz. 16 dwt. 18 gr. Among the articles recently deposited in the Museum by the Royal Dublin Society, there is a brass model of a gold torque, with plain conical ends, which measures 12½ inches in diameter; and in the *Vetusta Monumenta*, vol. v., pl. 29, may be seen engravings of two gold torques of this description, found in Ireland, each about 9½ inches in diameter, which were in the possession of the Earl of Charleville in 1819.

Another description of torque, evidently from its size a Neck-ring—*Muin-torc,* or *Muinche*—consists of a simple flat strip or band of gold, the breadth of a piece of ordinary tape, loosely twisted, and having generally small hooked extremities, which loop into one another. Of this kind there are three very perfect specimens and many fragments in the Collection. Nos. 181 and 182 are of nearly the same size and weight, the former of which, Figure 601, in the foregoing illustration, is a typical example. It measures 5½ inches in diameter, and weighs 19 dwt. 16 gr. No. 291, in Case F, figured half size, is a very fine specimen of the same variety, recently found with No. 290, near Clonmacnoise (see page 47); but differs from those already referred to, in having hollow, olive-shaped terminations. The twisted portion

---

Transactions, vol. xviii., p. 181. For a learned and ingenious Essay on the Torques of the Celts, see Mr. Birch's paper in the Archæological Journal, vols. ii. and iii.

is not so well finished as in the corresponding articles in Case **E**, already referred to; but it possesses an especial interest from being the only torque which has yet come to light which tends to explain a passage in one of our ancient ma-

Fig. 603. No. 291.

nuscripts, describing " two apples or balls of gold on the two forks of his *muinche* [neck-torque], each the size of a man's fist."* It measures 5½ inches across, and weighs 2 oz. 2 dwt. 5 gr.†—*Presented by the Government.*

Of the same form of light, flexible neck ornament, but still more attenuated and fragile, and somewhat more complex

---

* Irish MS., H. 3. 18, p. 391, in the Library of Trinity College. quoted by Dr. Petrie, in his Essay on the History and Antiquities of Tara Hill, Trans. R. I. A., vol. xviii., p. 183.

† There is a small torque of this variety in the Antiquarian Museum of Edinburgh, of which there is a model in the Comparative and Illustrative Collection of the Academy.

in construction, are the fragments of at least seven small torques, arranged at the bottom of Case **E**, each composed of a screw-shaped and exquisitely thin band, broad in the centre, and tapering gradually towards the ends, where it terminated either in small hooks or button-shaped projections, as represented in the three subjoined cuts, drawn, the full size, from Nos. 197, 198, and 202. The most

Fig. 604. No. 197.   Fig. 605. No. 198.   Fig. 606. No. 202.

of these fragments vary from 1 to 2 inches in length; several are much smaller, but have been joined together by means of fine gold-wire. The remains of these seven torques weigh but 2 oz. 10 dwt. 11 gr.; and the majority of them were found at Derravonna, near Crom Castle, county of Fermanagh. See details at page 80.*

While most of these neck-torques are so light, elegant, and fragile, as only to be found in fragments, like the remains of the spiral specimens, portions of

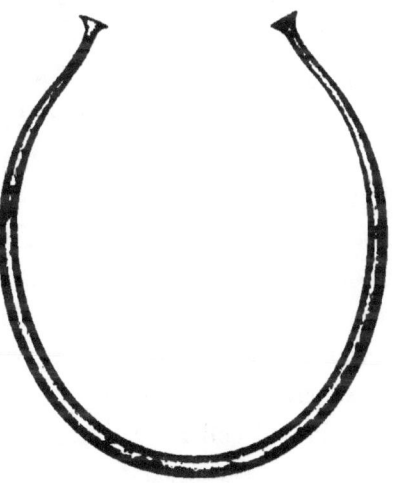

Fig. 607. No. 175.

which are figured above, others are solid, perfectly plain, either round or flat in section, and oval in form, as shown by the annexed illustration from No. 175, one of a pair which

---

* That learned antiquary, Mr. Albert Way, in his valuable article on "Ancient Armillæ of Gold," in vol. vi. of the Archæological Journal, for 1849, p. 53, has figured and described one of these beautiful ornaments, "formed of a thin plate or riband of gold, skilfully twisted, the spiral line being preserved with singular pre-

formed a part of the "Clare Find," already referred to at page 31. It is 6¼ inches across, and 6⅜ in the long diameter, and is formed of a circular bar, thick in the middle, and tapering to the button-shaped and slightly everted extremities, which are 3 inches apart. It weighs 6 oz. 12 dwt., or 1 dwt. 18 gr. less than its fellow, No. 176, described at page 79.

Although the use and mode of application of the flexible twisted bands, or neck-torques, already referred to, is so apparent as to leave no room for speculation, the manner of wearing the thick, heavy gold twisted ring, with wide-spread ends, No. 174, represented by Figure 602, in the general torque illustration at page 71, is not so manifest. It is 25 inches in length, is 5¾ in diameter, measures 7¾ between the terminal ends, and weighs 12 oz. 10 dwt. 7 gr. The roping resembles a coil of several wires; but the everted terminations are plain, and enlarged towards their ends. It was found in May, 1841, three feet under the surface, near Aughrim, in the neighbourhood of Ballinasloe, county of Galway.

Of the torque-pattern armlets, an example has been afforded by Figure 585, at page 53; and of the finger-rings, which assume that shape, No. 184, figured at page 81, is a good specimen. No. 188, in Case E, here shown, the natural size, by Figure 608, is a portion of torque, formed of four wires, twisted together, and encircled at the end by a decorated collar. It weighs 5 dwt. 15 gr.

Fig. 608. No. 188.

This fragment was cut off sharp, as if with a chisel, and now measures only 2⅛ inches, but its workmanship is particularly elegant. Its

---

cision," which was found at Largo, in Fifeshire, near the Frith of Forth, and which Mr. Dundas, of Arniston, its owner, regarded as of Danish origin. No such ornaments have, however, been found in any part of Scandinavia; and Mr. Way very justly remarks—"we are reluctant to suppose so graceful an ornament to be of Danish origin." Had this Catalogue been published fourteen years ago, the English and Scotch antiquaries would have had no difficulty in assigning an Irish origin to these ornaments.

analysis shows it to consist of gold, 96·90; silver, 2·49; and copper, a trace. See Transactions, R. I. A., vol. xxii., p. 34, No. 3.

Besides the various uses to which the golden torque of the Irish was applied, as explained in the foregoing description, it was probably also worn on the head, or for binding up the hair; in which position it may have been an emblem of royalty or power. It is stated that when Julian the Apostate was proclaimed emperor by the soldiers, one of them, named Maurus (probably a Gaulish Celt), took the torque from his neck, and placed it on the head of the monarch.*

It is related in the Book of Ballymote that, when Cormac Mac Art reigned at Tara, he wore a fine purple garment, had a golden brooch on his breast, and a *muin-torc*, or collar of gold, around his neck, and a belt adorned with gold and precious stones about him.†

In that part of the Life of St. Brendan, of Clonfert, referring to his visit to the monks of Meath, we read that Dermot Mac Cerrbheoil, the last resident king at Tara, saw in a dream two angels, who took his torque from his neck, and gave it to a stranger. When the king saw St. Brendan, he exclaimed, " This is the man to whom the angels gave my

---

* See Gibbon's Decline and Fall of the Roman Empire, A. D. 300. The words used by the great historian are :—Julian " was exalted on a shield in the presence and amidst the unanimous acclamations of the troops ; a rich military collar, which was offered by chance, supplied the want of a diadem." In the edition of Gibbon published in Bohn's British Classics, "with variorum notes; edited, with further illustratrations from the most recent sources, by an English Churchman," we find in vol. ii., at p. 470, the following most extraordinary note :—" Even in this tumultuous moment, Julian attended to the forms of superstitious ceremony, and obstinately refused the inauspicious use of a female necklace, or a horse-collar, which the impatient soldiers would have employed in the room of a diadem." Why the Editor should have thought it necessary to dispute the text of Gibbon, and the authorities on which the great English writer relied, and called the " rich military collar" nothing more than " a female necklace, *or* a horse-collar," it is difficult to imagine.

† See Petrie's History and Antiquities of Tara Hill, Transactions, R. I. A., vol. xviii., p. 183.

torque." The dream was interpreted by the sages, that his kingdom should pass away from him, and become the inheritance of clerics.*

The celebrated statue of the dying gladiator has a torque round the neck; and in the Pompeian mosaic referred to at p. 311, Vol. I., the chief equestrian figure is decorated with a torque round the neck, and torques on the arms, between the shoulders, and elbows. When Cornelius overcame the Boii, an ancient Gaulish people, no less than 1470 torques were collected from the vanquished. The term Torquatus was bestowed on Titus Manlius and his posterity, on account of the golden torque which he took from a Celtic Gaul. The ancient British queen, Boadicea, is described as having been decorated with this form of ornament; and subsequent to her time, a " Welsh prince was called *Llewellin aur dorchag*, or Llewellin of the golden torque."

Alluding to a very early period of Irish bardic history, Keating says, "at this time there was a *Fleasc*, or bracelet, on the arm of every chieftain, as a mark of dignity as leader of a sept; and hence, at this day, the head of a tribe is called in Irish *Fleascach Uasal*."† The same Irish historian states that, in the chivalrous days of the Knights of the Red Branch, and the renowned Queen Meabdh, of Connaught—the times of the *Tain Bo Cuailgne*, or great cattle-raid of Ulster—" It was the custom, as an inducement to champions to behave valiantly in the fight, to give the badge of heroes [*mir curadh*] as a mark of victory, to him who showed himself the bravest in single combat, and who vanquished his adversary in the field of valour;" and, adds the translator in a note, "it was some ornament or mark of merit, like the medals or ribbands of modern times."—p. 377.

The celebrated Ollam Mac Liag, the poet laureate of

---

* See *Codex Kilkenniensis*, in Archbishop Marsh's Library; also Petrie's Tara, *loc. cit.*

† See Haliday's Keating, vol. i., p. 237.

Brian Boroihme, gives an account in the Leabhar Oiris of an excursion which he made to the plain of Rath Raithlen, when both himself and his attendants were presented with a variety of gifts—kine, horses, and armour, garments, chess-tables, and also chains, rings, and many ounces of gold.*

The following is a detailed list of the various articles of the torque pattern in Case **E**:—

Case **E** contains thirty-six articles of the torque pattern, numbered from 171 to 207, among which are the two great torques found at Tara. Nos. 171 and 172 are a pair of twisted unclosed bracelets, found with No. 90, in Case **C**, and Nos. 273 and 279, in Case **F**, in the county of Carlow, in 1858. The first measures $2\frac{3}{4}$ inches in diameter, and weighs 12 dwt. 3 gr. The second is figured and described at p. 53. No. 173 is the smaller of the Tara torques, figured and described at pp. 71 and 72. No. 174 (within the former), the massive neck-torque, with recurved ends, figured and described at pp. 71 and 76. Nos. 175 and 176, placed on opposite sides of the case, a pair of plain oval neck-torques, of a peculiar pattern, and almost identical in shape, size, and weight. The former is figured and described at pp. 75 and 76. The latter is $6\frac{1}{4}$ inches wide, and $6\frac{3}{4}$ in the long diameter; Wt., 6 oz. 13 dwt. 18 gr. They were found together, and form a portion of the "Clare find." No. 177, a small penannular torque-shaped bar, $\frac{1}{8}$ inch wide, square in section; Wt., 2 dwt. 7 gr. No. 178, ditto, on opposite side of Case, somewhat larger; Wt., 5 dwt. (Dawson). No. 179, a light, but very elegant waist-torque, the third largest in the Collection, of the screw or spiral pattern, like No. 173; solid conical terminations; measures $44\frac{1}{2}$ inches in length, of which each terminal loop is $2\frac{1}{2}$;

---

* See Hardiman's Irish Minstrelsy, vol. ii., p. 371.

Before concluding the description of the chief personal ornaments of gold, the following additional references to the *Mind*, for which I am indebted to Mr. Crowe, already referred to at p. 12, serve still further to illustrate this interesting subject:—
"It was Fallaman's vow that he would not go back to Eman, until he should bring the head of Ailell with him, together with the *Mind* of gold which was on it "—*Tain Bo Cuailgne*, L. H., fol. 56. B. "Let the Druid go in my figure, says Ailell, and the *Mind* of a king upon his head."—*Ibid.*, fol. 53.

diameter, 13; Wt., 3 oz. 3 dwt. 15 gr. (Sirr). No. 180, a very remarkable waist-ring, of the torque shape, but quadrilateral in section, each face of the square being $\frac{3}{10}$ of an inch broad, with round hooked terminations, each $1\frac{1}{2}$ inches long; measures $37\frac{1}{2}$ inches in length, and $10\frac{3}{4}$ in diameter of circle; Wt., 9 oz. 16 dwt 18 gr. Found, with No. 186, in the vicinity of Enniscorthy, county of Wexford, and purchased by a subscription from the Members of the Royal Irish Academy. No. 181, the light and beautifully-twisted neck-torque (Fig. 601), forming a portion of the group represented and described at p. 71 (Dawson). No. 182, ditto, smaller, but of the same character, and 5 inches across the circle; button-shaped hooked terminations; Wt., 17 dwt. 12 gr. No. 183, small terminal fragment of a torque; Wt., 8 dwt. No. 184, a small plain, three-sided bar of gold, flat internally, angular externally, twisted spirally; probably used as a finger-ring; $1\frac{1}{4}$ inches in diameter. It has been figured and described at p. 81. No. 185, a flat neck-torque, formed out of a rudely hammered bar of gold, with very small terminal knobs; measures $5\frac{1}{8}$ inches in diameter, and $1\frac{1}{2}$ across the opening; Wt., 3 oz. 9 dwt. 9 gr. No. 186, a circular torque, round in section of bar, perfectly plain, $16\frac{1}{2}$ inches long, $5\frac{5}{8}$ wide, and $1\frac{1}{2}$ across the opening; Wt., 5 oz. 4 dwt. 6 gr. It was found with No. 180. No. 187, the fragment of a small twisted torque, similar to, but rather smaller in grist than No. 179; length $3\frac{1}{4}$ inches; Wt., 4 dwt. 19 gr. No. 188, a fragment of a torque, figured and described at p. 76. No. 189, a very slender, twisted neck-torque, of the same pattern as No. 179, quite perfect, with small hooked terminations; $5\frac{1}{8}$ inches in diameter; Wt., 12 dwt. 14 gr. (Dawson). No. 190, a small torque, square in section of bar, but twisted; probably a finger-ring, unclosed; 1 inch in diameter; Wt., 3 dwt. 9 gr. No. 191, a penannular armlet, figured and described at p. 52. No. 192, the great Tara torque, figured and described at p. 71. No. 193, placed within the former, the massive gold ring, Fig. 574, described at p. 46. No. 194, a penannular armilla, slightly bent, figured at p. 52.

On each side of the bottom of this Tray have been arranged a collection of remarkably thin twisted neck-torques, none of them perfect; but the whole, although in numerous fragments, may be divided into the remains of seven distinct torques. They are numbered from 195 to 207.

No. 195, the centre portion of a twisted torque; Wt., 1 dwt. 19 gr. No. 196, four portions of similar articles, wired together; Wt., 5 oz. 15 gr. No. 197, the end portion of a twisted neck-torque, with button-shaped termination, formed of an extremely thin ribbon of gold, very curiously twisted; Wt., 5 dwt. 6 gr. figured and described at p. 75. No. 198, ditto, with small hook termination; Wt., 4 dwt. 10 gr.; figured and described at p. 75. No. 199, ditto, larger, probably about a third of its original length; hook turned backwards; Wt., 6 dwt. 10 gr. No. 200, ditto, has neither hook nor button termination; Wt., 7 dwt. 10 gr. No. 201, the end portions of a slight torque, with hooked terminations; Wt., 23 gr. No. 202, ditto, larger; Wt., 1 dwt. 6 gr.; figured and described at p. 75. No. 203, portions of torques, wired together; Wt., 3 dwt. 21 gr. No. 204, ditto; Wt., 3 dwt. 18 gr. No. 205, ditto; Wt., 3 dwt. 9 gr. No. 206, ditto; Wt., 2 dwt. 17 gr. No. 207, ditto; Wt., 3 dwt. 15 gr.

FINGER-RINGS—in Irish, *Fainne*—of gold, many of which are jewelled, have been found in Ireland in great variety, but few are of antique origin; several of them are ecclesiastical. With one exception, they are all arranged in Case F, and numbered from 208 to 257. See their detailed description at page 92. Of the more ancient forms, the first two cuts in

Fig. 609.   No. 252.   Fig. 610.   No. 184.   Fig. 611.   No. 227.

the annexed illustration are good examples. Figure 609, represented the full size, from No. 252, in Case F, is like a ferule, fluted both externally and internally, so as to resemble seven plain rings attached together. It is open at one side, and weighs 9 dwt.* Figure 610, drawn the full size, from No. 184, in Case E, is a five-sided bar of gold, flat on the inside next the finger, and angular externally, weighing 1 oz. 12 dwt. 6 gr. It may be denominated a torque-ring. The third cut, Figure 611, is drawn from No. 227, a comparatively modern article, evidently a bishop's ring. It is said that it originally held a very fine amethyst, which was removed by Dean Dawson, when the article was in his possession, and a piece of glass inserted in its stead. The total number of gold finger-rings in the Collection at present is fifty.

SPECIES XI.—MISCELLANEOUS.

CIRCULAR GOLD PLATES, of which there are seven specimens in the Collection, placed in Case F, and numbered from 266 to 272, are of frequent occurrence in Ireland, an example of which is afforded by Figure 612, drawn, half size, from No. 267. They are remarkably thin, very rudely decorated, always bear a broad cruciform ornament in the centre, and are pierced with two small holes, as if for attaching them to the dress. They are often found in pairs, and were probably worn on the breast. In dimensions they vary from $1\frac{3}{8}$ to $3\frac{3}{4}$ inches, and in weight from about 2 to 13 pennyweights. That here figured is $3\frac{1}{4}$ inches in diameter, and weighs 5 dwt. 18 gr. The ornamentation appears to have been effected by stamping from the back. It was found, with No. 271, near Ballina, county Mayo, and was procured for the Academy by the Rev. Dr. Todd. A peculiar interest attaches to these articles, from the remarkable circumstance related by Bishop Gibson, in his

---

* A precisely similar ring, but somewhat smaller and lighter, was found at Rathfarnham, near Dublin, in 1855, and was figured and described by Captain E. Hoare, as a specimen of "ring-money," in the Journal of the Kilkenny and S. E. of Ireland Archæological Society, vol. i., N. S., p. 391, for 1856-57.

edition of Camden's Britannia, of the discovery of those described by him in 1722. Shortly before that period, Dr. Nicolson, Bishop of Derry, when dining at Ballyshannon, county of Donegal, was entertained by an Irish harper, whose song detailed the burial in a certain place of a gigantic man, adorned with golden ornaments. To test the accuracy of the bard's narration, search was immediately made in the spot, when two thin, circular gold plates, like these under consideration, were discovered, and one of which has been figured by Gibson. Another of the same class has been represented in the Dublin Penny Journal, vol. i., p. 244, by Dr. Petrie, who says:—" The figures of the kings sculptured in *relievo* on the great stone cross at Clonmacnoise are represented with round plates of this description, placed upon the breast."

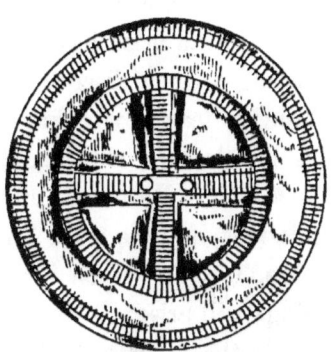

Fig. 612. No. 267.

Among the objects of personal decoration attached to the dress, or strung on necklaces, and which have been found great numbers in Scandinavia, particularly in Denmark and Sweden, are Bracteate medals, mostly of Grecian or Oriental origin, generally plain on one side, but stamped with a variety of devices on the other; and having a loop at top for the purpose of suspension. One such article, No. 263, in Case F, here figured, the size of the original, has been found in Ireland,—probably left by the Norsemen. It is a medal of Constantine, in high preservation, plain on the obverse side, and weighing 2 dwt. 13 gr. The legend is " IMPerator CONSTANTINVS Pius Felix AVGustus," and the portrait is probably that of Constantine the First.

Fig. 613. No. 263.

CIRCULAR BOXES, supposed by some to have been used

for *mortuary* purposes, have been occasionally found in Ireland, and are represented by two perfect specimens, and fragments of three others, in the Museum of the Academy; but the circumstances under which the former were discovered have not been clearly ascertained. Heretofore the finders of golden antiquities have endeavoured to conceal all the facts relating to their discovery, or the articles have been obtained through dealers who knew nothing of the circumstances, or from collectors, who cared merely for their acquisition and possession. But now, under the existing treasure-trove regulations, and the more general diffusion of antiquarian knowledge, it may reasonably be hoped that a better order of things will arise.

By the subjoined illustration is represented one of those boxes, one-half the natural size, from No. 275, in Case **F**. It is composed of three portions, two circular convex discs, of very thin gold plates, embossed with a large central ornament, surrounded by two rows of minor ones of the same character, and precisely resembling those on the College fibula, shown by Figure 593, page 60,—associating it with that very early style of Irish art, the first rudiments of which may be seen in some of the rudely incised stones in the great sepulchral monuments of New Grange. The edge is encircled with a rope-shaped fillet, beyond which the plate turns in to interlap with and affix the rim, which it holds without solder. The rim or side is also of very thin plate, plain in the middle, but decorated near each edge by a double funiform band of the same pattern as that in the top or lid, and the extreme edges plain, and interlapping with the top and bottom plates. The side meets by an accurately adjusted but unsoldered junction, as shown in the engraving. The bottom disc, No. 274, in nowise differs from the upper in the style

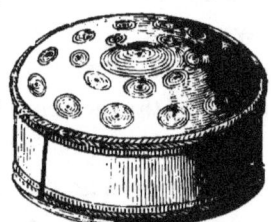

Fig. 614. No. 275.

of its ornament. The weight of the whole article, including the lower plate, is 19 dwt. 11 gr. It is asserted that the armilla, No. 114, in Case D, was found in this box. The second box, No. 277, with its bottom, No. 278, is identical in character, and presents almost the same style of ornament.

With the two torque-shaped armillæ, Nos. 171 and 172, in Case E, described at pages 53 and 79, and other similar ornaments found in the county Carlow, in 1858, were discovered four thin grooved plates, two of which, Nos. 273 and 279, are in Case F, and the latter of which is here figured, one-half the real size. The fluting is as regular as if effected by machinery, and each edge is mar-

Fig. 615. No. 279.

gined by a double raised fillet, beyond which the extreme verge is very thin, and slightly everted. It weighs 12 dwt. 4 gr. These articles were at first sight believed to have been bracelets; but a more careful examination, and comparison with the rims of the circular boxes referred to above, now explains their use.

BULLÆ, or AMULETS, composed of lead, and covered with highly decorated gold plates, are not of uncommon occurrence in this country. They are of two kinds,—the heart-shaped and the annular, two fine specimens of each of which are now in the Collection of the Academy, Nos. 258, 259, 264, and 265, in Case F, all of which are here represented. Figure 616, drawn, the full size, from No. 264, is plain in the body, but neatly decorated round the edge, and also at top, where it is traversed by a hole for the passage of a string, or for suspending it to a necklace. Figure 617, No. 265, one-half

Fig. 616. No. 264.

the true size, represents one of the most beautiful articles of this variety ever discovered. Internally it is composed of lead, which is surrounded by a thin plate of gold, highly decorated with a different pattern on each side. It weighs 4 oz. 14 dwt. 12 gr. The style of ornament resembles that in some of the cinerary urns, and the earliest gold ornaments found in Ireland, but is much more regular, and exhibits a better order of art and workmanship than in most of the latter. It is traversed at top by a string-hole, and the joining of the golden envelope is so accurate as not to be discernible. It was found upwards of a century ago in the Bog of Allen, and was procured with the Dawson Collection.*

Fig. 617. No. 265.

The two unclosed rings, Figs. 618 and 619, drawn, the full size, from Nos. 258 and 259, are said to have been found in cinerary urns. They are also of lead, covered on the outside with ornamented gold plates,

Fig. 618. No. 258.

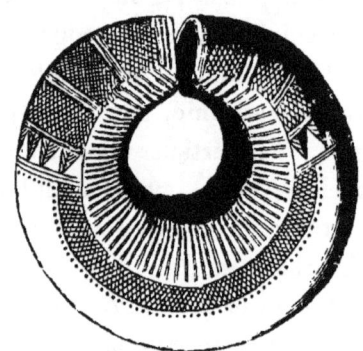
Fig. 619. No. 259.

the workmanship of which is, however, inferior to that in the heart-shaped amulets. Each ring narrows towards the cleft part, and the gold plate is merely turned in all round the top and bottom, as well as at the lateral edge, in a rudely plaited manner.

Not the least curious, and as yet one of the most inexplicable specimens arranged under the head of "Miscellaneous Articles," is the hat-shaped gold plate, No. 276, in Case F, and represented, half-size, by the accompanying illustration.

---

* See the description of it in the Dublin Penny Journal, vol. i., p. 180.

The plate is exceedingly thin, much crumpled, and grooved all round with circular indentations and elevations. It weighs 1 oz. 2 dwt. 2 gr. This article, which is manifestly imperfect, is a portion of the original Collection of the Academy, and is described by Ralph Ouseley, Esq., in 1795, in the Transactions, R. I. A., vol. vi., page 31, as forming one of four precisely similar articles, "quite circular, and 4¾ inches in diameter, very thin, ornamented handsomely at one side, and quite plain at the other, except a kind of cap or screw, for the purpose of being affixed to a handle." They were found in 1795, near Enniscorthy, county of Wexford. Two were melted, and the others, of which we believe this to be one, were sent "for sale to the Earl of Charlemont, President of our Academy."

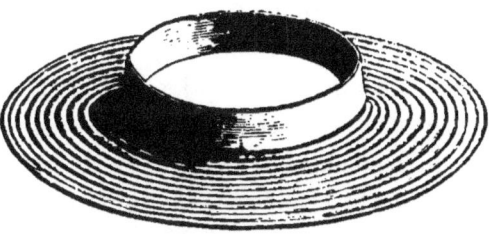

Fig. 620. No. 276.

For the description of the other gold articles in the Museum, not previously enumerated, see the details of Case F, at page 91.

RING-MONEY.—Although we cannot subscribe to the general theory of "ring-money," as applicable to bronze and iron articles, referred to at page 635 of Vol. I.,—to all of which, as well as to most of the gold and silver rings, can now be assigned a plainer and more ostensible use,—there are a number of small, thick, gold, penannular articles in the Collection, which may have been used *merely* as a means of barter, and which abound in all Irish collections. To no other use can they at present be assigned; and the fact that among them may be found several ancient counterfeits, formed of copper, covered with thin plates of gold, rather strengthens the idea that they were intended as a circulating medium. The Academy possesses fifteen such rings, arranged in a semicircle in Case **D**, together with five counterfeits, placed at its base, and also one in Case **F**. Those rings in the former locality are numbered from 151 to 170. In shape they are nearly all similar, and vary in diameter from ⅜ to ¾ of an inch. See their description at page 69.

Among the sterling rings may be seen three which present peculiar characters, being crossed by a number of dark-coloured transverse bars, which, when the specimen is in good preservation, or recently found, look like alternate rings of gold and *niello*, or some dark silvery metal, and give them a sort of zebra-marked appearance. On careful examination, however, with a lens, these stripes are found to consist of shallow indentations, filled with some dark material, like the black paste inserted by engravers into brass plates. In some rings portions of this material have fallen out, been worn away, or corroded: and then, the true nature of the decoration becomes apparent. The following cuts present us with four typi-

Fig. 621. No. 151.   Fig. 622. No. 159.   Fig. 623. No. 160.   Fig. 624. No. 287.

cal forms of these rings:—the small crescentic example, Fig. 621, fining off to the extremities, like Fig. 597, page 63, and weighing only 1 dwt. 12 gr.; the plain massive one, No. 159, Fig. 622, which weighs 10 dwt. 20 gr.; the striped example, No. 160, Fig. 623, weighing 8 dwt. 17 gr.; and the counterfeit, Fig. 624, from No. 285, on Case **F**, in which the covering-plate of gold is shown at one point turned back from the copper beneath. This latter weighs 8 dwt. 10 gr., and was —*Presented by W. R. Wilde, Esq.* It is very remarkable that, while the joining of this golden envelope cannot be discovered along its edge or length, it is in all instances very rudely and ostensibly bent in and hammered over the ends of the copper, without any effort at concealment. In the sterling rings, the ends are not cut sharply off, but neatly rounded, and well finished. A comparison of the weights of these rings does not favour the arguments used by the supporters of the ring-money theory; for they not only present great variety in their weights, but do not show any scale of proportion from the largest to the least; neither are they, nor any description of so-called ring-money, multiples of twelve or of any other definite number.*

As the nucleus of all these antique counterfeits is copper, and not bronze, and as the latter metal was not known until long after the discovery of gold and copper, it suggests the inquiry as to whether it was in use in Ireland when these penannular articles were manufactured.

The subject of ring-money will be further considered in the introduction to the catalogue of the coins and medals.

Within the last few months several rare and valuable antique gold articles have been discovered in Ireland, and are now in the Collection of the Royal Irish Academy. See pages 47, 74, and 95. Of these, No. 306, in Case E, is one of the

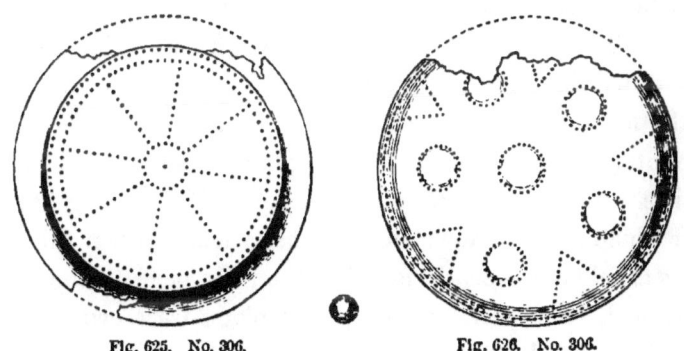

Fig. 625. No. 306.   Fig. 626. No. 306.

most remarkable. This unique article, represented two-thirds the real size by the above woodcut, consists of four very thin,

---

* Sir W. Betham figured some of these rings from the Dawson Collection. See Trans. R. I. A., vol. xvii.; and also his *Etruria Celtica*.

circular plates, two small in front, and two somewhat larger behind; the whole joined together in the following manner: The anterior small plate, shown in Fig. 625, is 2¾ inches in diameter, and decorated with a wheel-shaped ornament, produced by a series of minute puncturings from behind, not unlike those seen in the circular plates, Nos. 266, 270, and 272, and of which variety of article the illustration of a typical specimen is afforded by Fig. 612, at p. 83. The edge of this plate is turned back for about one-eighth of an inch to overlap and attach it to the second plate, of same size, but plain and considerably stronger. This second plate has a large irregularly circular aperture in the middle, about seven-eighths of an inch wide, which interlaps, and is firmly united with the edges of a similar opening in the third plate. This latter is also plain, stout towards the centre, and about a quarter of an inch all round wider than the foregoing; its thin edge is overlapped by the fourth or posterior plate in the same manner as the two others. In both the overlapment is precisely similar to that in the bosses of the diadems described at pp. 20 and 23, &c. The fourth or posterior plate, represented by Fig. 626, is of the same size as the last, and decorated with the same form of punched ornament, but of a different pattern to that seen in the small anterior disc, and, in addition, having originally the spaces within the small circles elevated from the surrounding plate, not unlike those seen in Box No. 275 (see p. 94). In the interspace between the central plates was found, when the article was discovered, a small solid gold ball, weighing 11 gr., and which is also shown in the illustration. When this curious article was recently found in the plain beneath the Rock of Cashel, county of Tipperary, the plates were crushed flat together, and there are the indentations in both the external plates of three such balls. When this article was complete, the outer plates were probably convex externally, like the lateral discs of the diadems, and these little balls may have been introduced to produce a rattle. It is now much crushed and battered, but the anterior plate is still partially, and the two central ones altogether, united. When perfect, there must have been a deep angular groove externally between the middle plates. The use of this curious relic cannot be determined with any degree of certainty. The very early style of art, and the absence of all cruciform decoration, leads us to believe that it was not employed for ecclesiastical purposes, but was either a toy or a personal ornament, possibly an ear-ring. For the latter object, or for suspending to the dress, a string passed round the cleft between the middle plates would suffice; and as both external plates are equally adorned, it is more likely to have been attached to the ear. Thus we see that every day produces new and hitherto unknown forms of our ancient jewellery. It weighs 11 dwt. 3 gr., and was procured under the present treasure-trove regulations, and—*Presented by the Government.*

Of gold chains, such as those with which Muineamhon decorated the Irish chieftains in his day (see Annals of the Four Masters, under A.M., 3872), and now very rarely discovered, we have as yet no specimen in the collection; but Lord Londesborough, in his magnificent work,* has figured one found at New Grange, county Meath.

The total number of gold articles now in the Academy's Museum, including the additional gold ball, No. 36, A, recently procured, amounts, at this date (1st March, 1862), to three hundred and ten.

Case F contains a collection of miscellaneous articles, numbered from 208 to 309, and chiefly consisting of finger-rings, boxes, discs,

---

* Miscellanea Graphica. Representations of Ancient Mediæval and Renaissance Remains, in the possession of Lord Londesborough. London, 1857, 4to. Plate xvii., Fig. 3, a chain found along with several other gold articles.

Mr. A. C. Welsh, of Dromore, possesses a curious pyriform plate, with a narrow stem, which may have been used as an ear ring.—See a drawing thereof in the illustrative Collection of the Academy.

bullæ, &c. No. 208, a small gold finger-ring, decorated in front, and bearing a Maltese cross in white and dark-coloured enamel; Wt., 1 dwt. 1 gr. No. 209, ditto, irregular in shape, sides elaborately carved; sapphire stone; Wt., 1 dwt. 9 gr. (Sirr). No. 210, ditto, with large pale sapphire; Wt., 1 dwt. 18 gr. No. 211, ditto, plain, thick, with central projection, bearing a small, rudely-set sapphire (probably ecclesiastical); Wt., 4 dwt. 3 gr. No. 212, ditto, with small triangular sapphire; Wt., 2 dwt. 5 gr. No. 213, ditto, more massive, sapphire lozenge-shaped; Wt., 3 dwt. 15 gr. No. 214, ditto, thinner, small tourmaline (ecclesiastical); Wt., 2 dwt. 19 gr. No. 215, ditto, a long oval, sapphire small; Wt., 3 dwt. 4 gr. No. 216, ditto, sapphire heart-shaped; Wt., 4 dwt. 11 gr. No. 217, finger-ring, with carved hoop and purple stone; Wt., 1 dwt. 6 gr. No. 218, ditto, with a garnet cut with five faces, in massive setting; Wt., 1 dwt. 21 gr.; procured from county of Waterford (Sirr). No. 219, ditto, small, with large raised setting, holding an uncut pinkish stone; Wt., 2 dwt. 17 gr.—*Presented by the Rev. W. Fitzgerald.* No. 220, ditto, very small, plain hoop, and turquoise stone; Wt., 23 gr. Second Row :—No. 221, an antique ring, decorated with a number of knobs; Wt., 1 dwt. 8 gr. No. 222, ditto, hoop plain, holding an irregular-shaped uncut garnet, set clear: Wt., 1 dwt. 23 gr. No. 223, ditto, massive, battered in setting part; Wt., 7 dwt. 8 gr. No. 224, a thumb or large finger-ring, the carved hoop holds an antique gem; Wt., 5 dwt. 21 gr. (Sirr). No. 225, a finger-ring, with uncut pink stone; Wt., 2 dwt. 4 gr. No. 226, a beautiful and elaborately ornamented finger-ring, with massive setting, holding an uncut garnet; Wt., 2 dwt. 22 gr. No. 227, the largest ring in the Collection, figured and described at p. 81. No. 228, a highly decorated ring, beryl stone; Wt., 4 dwt. 8 gr. (Sirr). No. 229, a peculiarly formed small ring, like a seal, with three uncut stones; Wt., 3 dwt. 1 gr. No. 230, a finger-ring, with hoop enamelled in white, green, and blue, and holding four garnets set round a table diamond; Wt., 2 dwt. 9 gr.—*Presented by the Shannon Commissioners.* No. 231, ditto, small, with jet cross, and central diamond; Wt., 12 gr. No. 232, an enamelled mourning ring, with four scroll compartments, bearing the inscription, "Lord Bowes, died July 22, 1687;" he was Lord Chancellor of Ireland, and his monument is in Christ Church Cathedral; Wt., 2 dwt. 13 gr. No. 233, a mourning ring for "Sarah King;" Wt., 1 dwt. 3 gr. Third Row:—No. 234, gold signet-ring, with monogram; Wt., 7 dwt. 15 gr. No. 235, ditto, letters I. D., and device on face; Wt., 7 dwt. 17 gr. No. 236, ditto, with skull and crossbones, and the words, "*Memento mori;*" Wt., 7 dwt. 19 gr. No. 237, ditto, large, with coat of arms; Wt., 11 dwt. 8 gr. No. 238, ditto, ditto; Wt., 5 dwt. 13 gr. No. 239, ditto, with crest and letters W. C. M.; Wt., 8 dwt. 9 gr. (Dawson). No. 240, ditto, crest, a hand and dagger; Wt., 6 dwt. 6 gr. (Dawson). No. 241, a thick gold hoop, with clasped hands supporting a heart; Wt., 6 dwt. 4 gr.; from county of Limerick (Sirr). No. 242, ditto, large, hoop plain, clasped hands; Wt., 3 dwt. 3 gr. No. 243, ditto; Wt., 3 dwt. 16 gr. No. 244, gold hoop, with crucifix; Wt., 1 dwt. 12 gr. No. 245, a decade ring, with sunken crucifix in central oval; Wt., 21 gr. No. 246, a decade ring, with cypher; Wt., 15 gr. Fourth Row:—No. 247, a plain hoop, with motto inside, "God's intent none can prevent;" Wt., 4 dwt. 4 gr.—*Presented by Maurice O'Connell, Esq.* No. 248, a plain ring of reddish gold, with the word "Crohan" engraved on the inside; probably of Wicklow gold; Wt., 1 dwt. 14 gr. See p. 5. No. 249, a hollow hoop, with floral wreath; Wt., 6 dwt. 11 gr. No. 250, a plain broad hoop; Wt., 6 dwt. 7 gr.; supposed to have been a ferule for the handle of a bronze dagger, with which it was found— *Presented by Maurice O'Connell, Esq.* No. 251, a decorated hoop, with cross and letters I. H. S.; Wt., 1 dwt. 7 gr. No. 252, a grooved ring or ferule, figured at p. 81. No. 253, a flat hoop, of very yellow gold, like No. 249; Wt., 6 dwt. 23 gr. No. 254, a plain thick hoop, with this inscription on inside, "Stand fast in faith;" Wt., 5 dwt. 8 gr. (Dawson). No. 255, a plain hoop, "1740, H. V. M.," on inside; Wt., 2 dwt. 10 gr. Fifth Row:—No. 256, fragment of gold ring, with three knobs, like those of bronze, figured and described at p. 563, Vol. I.; Wt., 7 dwt. 21 gr. No. 257, a curious twisted leaden ring, plated with gold, probably not Irish. No. 258, a bulla of lead, covered with gold, figured and described at p. 86. No. 259, ditto, larger, and more perfect, figured and described at p. 86. No. 260, a semicircular hollow band, of highly ornamented gold, incomplete in two portions, resembling in form and decoration some of the silver ornaments; possibly of foreign origin. A portion of the original lead that filled the interior still remains; probably part of a head-dress; length $8\frac{1}{4}$ inches; Wt., 1 oz. 4 dwt. 2 gr. No. 261, a heart-shaped reliquary of gold, pierced, and highly enamelled in crimson, white, and green; probably foreign; watch-like handle and loop; length $2\frac{3}{8}$ inches; Wt., 1 oz. 2 dwt. 11 gr. Found at Howth (Sirr). No. 262, a highly decorated, but comparatively modern brooch, with four settings for stones; Wt., 5 dwt. 5 gr. No. 263, a gold medal, figured and described at p. 83. No. 264, a small bulla, figured and described at p. 85. No. 265, the large bulla, figured and described at p. 86. No. 266, a thin circular plate, $3\frac{3}{4}$ inches wide, with central cross, and two holes, possibly for attaching it to the dress; Wt., 13 dwt. 20 gr. Its match, No. 272, is placed on the opposite end of the row. No. 267, ditto, figured and described at p. 83. No. 268, ditto, ornament raised, with small square cross in centre; $2\frac{1}{4}$ inches wide; Wt., 4 dwt. 17 gr. (Sirr). No. 269, ditto, the smallest in the Collection, imperfect; $1\frac{3}{8}$ inches in diameter; Wt., 2 dwt. 2 gr. No. 270, ditto, large, but very thin; $2\frac{5}{8}$ inches across; Wt., 4 dwt. 12 gr. (Dawson). No. 271, ditto; $3\frac{1}{8}$ inches across; Wt., 4 dwt. 10 gr.; found with No. 267. No. 272, ditto, the match of No. 266; Wt., 13 dwt. 10 gr. See p. 82. Seventh Row:—No. 273, the unclosed rim of a circular box, fluted on external surface, very thin; $\frac{3}{4}$ inch wide; $7\frac{3}{8}$ in length; Wt., 11 dwt. 16 gr. Found with the bracelets, Nos. 90, 171, and 172, in the county of Carlow. See its fellow, No. 279, on the opposite side. No. 274, the cover of the circular box, No. 275, marked with slight circular indentations, roped round edge; diameter $2\frac{5}{8}$ inches; Wt., 5 dwt. 9 gr. Found with the adjoining gold box, and is evidently its lid. No. 275, a circular gold box, consisting of lateral rim, and bottom similar to the foregoing, figured and described at p. 84. In it is said to have been found the bracelet, No. 114, in Case **D**. No. 276, a hat-shaped piece of thin gold, figured and described at pp. 86, 87. No. 277, a circular box, similar in size and ornament to No. 275; Wt., 14 dwt. 13 gr. In it is said to have been found the bracelet, No. 115, in Case **D**. No. 278, the cover or bottom of ditto; Wt., 5 dwt. 7 gr. No. 279, the fellow of No. 273, figured and described at p. 85. No. 280, a bar of wrought gold. See Fig. 580, p. 51. No. 281, a piece of thick gold-wire, bent, and cut off obliquely; Wt., 3 dwt. 12 gr. No. 282, a fragment of a massive cylindrical rod of wrought gold, 3¼ inches in length, to one end of which a small portion has been attached by hard solder (either for the purpose of the preservation of the latter, or possibly to make the whole a certain weight); Wt., 2 oz. 12 dwt. 9 gr. It was found in the county of Kildare; procured through Mr. West, as treasure-trove, and — *Presented by the Government.* No. 283, a gold ingot; figured and described at p. 51. No. 284, the large skewer-shaped bar of gold, figured and described at p. 51. No. 285, a small thin portion of gold plate; Wt., 10 gr. No. 286, two small fragments of a circular embossed gold plate; Wt., 12 gr. No. 287, the small copper and gold ring supposed to represent money; figured and described at p. 88. No. 288, a small spatula-shaped fragment of gold; Wt., 16 gr. Analyzed by Mallet, and found to consist of gold, 88.72; silver, 10·02; copper, 1·11; iron, ·02. Trans. R. I. A., Vol. xxii., p. 314. No. 289, four small fragments of wrought gold; Wt., 13 gr. No. 290, the large Scandinavian-shaped ring, figured and described at pp. 47 and 48. No. 291, the torque found with the former article, near Clonmacnoise. See Fig. 603, p. 74. No. 292, a thin flat plate of gold, smooth inside, grooved longitudinally on the external face like the rims of the boxes Nos. 273 and 279; it is 3⅛ inches long, by 13/16 wide; lateral edges plain, without overlapments; transverse edges much worn, and angles rounded off. The grooving is complete, and terminates at each extremity. When examined with a lens, it would appear as if the gouge-like tool with which this grooving was effected was lifted off the plate before it was carried to the extreme edge. This peculiarity is observable at both extremities, which are equally worn, showing that the article is complete; it is stated to have been found in a curved state; Wt., 5 dwt. 10 gr. No. 293, ditto, the fellow of the foregoing in every respect, except weight; Wt., 5 dwt. 20 gr. Both these articles were found together—procured under the treasure-trove minute, and—*Presented by the Government.* They are too short to have been used as the rims of boxes, and certainly bear no marks of having been cut or fractured; they are too thin to have retained the annular position as finger-rings. They are stated to have been found in the county of Tipperary, in the present year. Nos. 294 and 295 would appear to be portions of the same article, and to be identical with the box-rims, Nos. 273 and 279, the latter of which is figured at p. 85. Although apparently parts of the same article, the recently cut terminations do not match, a very small portion having been removed, the incision was quite recent when the articles were procured under the treasure-trove minute, and—*Presented by the Government* during the present month, February 1862. Each plate is plain on the inside, and grooved externally with an everted edge or overlapment, for attaching it to the turn-over of the top and bottom of a circular box, like No. 275, figured on p. 84. They are somewhat thicker towards the cut extremities (originally the middle) than at the other ends. A close examination of the termination of the grooving on these incomplete plates shows at once the difference between it and that in the two foregoing articles. Each plate is 4 inches long by $1\frac{3}{8}$ wide; when joined, they form a box-rim of the average size. The former weighs 6 dwt. 21 gr., and the latter 6 dwt. 10 gr. Nos. 296 to 305, a row of nine cylindrical beads, each formed of a fragment of thin plate of gold, rudely rolled upon itself, the row measuring 5 inches. Five are plain on both sides, and four grooved on the outer face, like Nos. 292 and 293, and are, most likely, fragments of similar articles. They may have been ferules for double conical beads, like that figured and described at p. 36; or they may have been worn with other trinkets on a necklace, or strung between amber beads. They somewhat resemble the row of cylindrical beads numbered from 42 to 47, in Case **C**, but are much ruder. In their present state they cannot be regarded as perfect; for the age and style of art which was capable of executing the minute and precise grooving on the surface of some of them would scarcely have left them in their present condition. The set weighs 5 dwt. 6 gr. No. 306, the curious quadruple set of circular plates figured and described at p. 89. See Figs. 625 and 626. No. 307, a penannular armilla, with cup-shaped terminations; bar cylindrical, thick in centre, and tapering towards extremities; very perfect; $2\frac{3}{4}$ inches in long diameter of oval; Wt., 1 oz. 2 dwt. 9 gr. No. 308, ditto, smaller, in fine preservation, with goblet-shaped terminations, like No. 111 in Case D ; bar cylindrical : encircling the edge of each cup is a slight fillet, which is worn away externally, showing that the article was there long subject to friction; 2½ inches in long diameter; Wt., 18 dwt. 15 gr. No. 309, ditto, bar cylindrical, and of equal grist throughout. It presents the rare peculiarity of having shallow oval cups, which are also partially unclosed at the bottom. The edges of the cups are very thin, and somewhat battered; measures 2⅝ inches in long diameter; Wt., 16 dwt. 8 gr. These three armillæ were found on the plain of Cashel, county of Tipperary; and, with Nos. 296 to 306, were procured under the treasure-trove authority, and—*Presented by the Government.*

In the enumeration of the various presents and tributes given in the Book of Rights, we read of gold-adorned shields and swords, of gold-trimmed cloaks and tunics, of "rings of red gold"—*fuilgibh derg oir;* and in one instance we find an entry of "a javelin with its mounting of wrought gold," as having formed part of the tribute to which the Chief of the Gaileanga, in Meath, was entitled. Even chariots were decorated with gold ;[*] and among the gifts said to have been offered to St. Patrick and his attendants was a "screapall[†] for each man,—an ounce of gold."[‡] When the Ultonian King of Emania visited the chief monarch at Tara, the latter was bound to present him with "the full breadth of his face of gold;" probably a *mind* or lunula. And, again, the King of

---

[*] See also the Annals of the Four Masters, under A. D. 9, in which the wonderful jewels of Crimhthann are enumerated. Among these was a golden chariot, a golden chess-board, a gold-embroidered cloak, and "a conquering sword with many serpents of refined massy gold inlaid in it."

[†] "*Screapall*, a coin used by the ancient Irish, weighing 24 gr., and of the value of three pence." See O'Donovan's translation of the Book of Rights, p. 228, *n.*, and Petrie's Round Towers, in Trans. R. I. A., vol. xx., p. 216 ; also Annals of Four Masters, under A. D. 1153.

[‡] A. D. 1004. Brian Boroihme left *twenty ounces* of gold as an offering on the altar of Armagh. By some commentators this mass of gold is said to have been in the form of a ring.—Ann. Four Masters.

Ui Gabhla was entitled to a ring of gold upon every finger; and a ring of gold, bright from the fire, was due to the fair King of the Forthuatha," in the territory of Imaile, in which the Church of Glendalough, in Wicklow, now stands. " Rings," in all likelihood of gold, and of different patterns, like those unclosed armillæ in the Academy's Collection, are frequently mentioned among the gifts and tributes presented to different other chieftains or petty kings, in return for the cattle-tax and refection for the troops of the provincial kings. The rings in other places are described as of " red gold," probably denoting the purity of the metal, " Drinking-horns on which is gold" are likewise enumerated in that remarkable work, to which reference has been frequently made in Vol. I. All these entries show the great amount of and the variety of purposes to which this precious metal was applied in the early days of barbaric splendour, and which the discoveries of subsequent times proves to be correct. See also the description and illustrations of the beautiful gold-covered bronze plates, given at pages 574 and 575, of Vol. I. The Druidic idols of the Pagan Irish are said to have been covered with plates of gold. The various shrines of early Christian times were adorned with this most precious but abundant metal; and the chalices and church furniture and decorations were of such splendour as to invite the plundering Norse across the wildest seas, and to have excited the cupidity of the Irish chieftains and their followers.* When, in addition

---

* The following extracts from O'Donovan's translation of the Annals of the Four Masters serve still further to illustrate this subject :—

A. D. 796. "The relics of Ronan, son of Bearach, were placed in a shrine of gold and silver."

A. D. 949. Godfrey, son of Sitric, with the Danes of Dublin, plundered Kells, and carried off "three thousand persons into captivity, besides, gold, silver, raiment," &c. Also An. Clonmacnoise.

A. D. 998. O'Melaghlin and Brian, son of Ceinneidigh, carried off the gold, silver, and prisoners of Dublin.

A. D. 1006. The great Gospel of Columbkille, or Book of Kells, was stolen from

to all these notices, we review the amount of gold procured by the Academy within the last thirty years, and of which only a few typical specimens have been engraved in this work; together with those preserved in the Londesborough and other Collections; and glance at the various records in different books, periodicals, and newspapers,* of articles long since lost to antiquarian investigation, and others known to have been melted down;—we think it must be acknowledged that we have established the position with which this section of the Catalogue was commenced, that no other country in Europe possesses so much manufactured gold belonging to early and mediæval times as Ireland.

Having in the foregoing pages enumerated and described the various gold ornaments which have been acquired by the Royal Irish Academy, and also endeavoured to establish the native origin and manufacture of these articles, it is with considerable diffidence that the author ventures to dissent from the opinion of the late President of the Academy, that "Geology assures us that there are no auriferous streams or veins of gold in Ireland, capable of supplying so very large a

the sacristy of that place. When discovered, it was found that the gold of its cover had been removed.

A. D. 1020. Armagh was burned by the Danes, with "much gold, silver, and other precious things."

A. D. 1129. The Church of Clonmacnoise was robbed, and among the stolen articles were several adorned with gold.

A. D. 1151. See page 7 of this Catalogue. For ten ounces, read "ten score ounces of gold."

A. D. 1157. At the consecration of Mellifont Abbey, in Louth, Murtagh O'Loughlin "presented seven score cows, and *three score ounces of gold*;" O'Carroll also "gave *three score ounces of gold*;" and Dearvorgil, the wife of O'Ruairc, "gave as much more, and a chalice of gold."

A. D. 1189. Hugh O'Conor gave Donnell O'Brien ten articles ornamented with gold.

* It is the author's intention to publish in the Proceedings a chronological account of the various Irish gold "finds" to which reference has been already made in the note at page 4.

mass of gold"* as would be required to furnish all the ornaments of that metal found at different times throughout the country, and a portion of which is now in the Museum. As already shown at page 4, geology proves that there are no less than seven localities in which gold has been found in Ireland; and the fact that upwards of £10,000 worth of gold was procured within a few weeks from one of these localities within the last eighty years, as already described at page 355 of Vol. I., and that in the very place where the annalists of old state that gold was first smelted and manufactured into ornaments, is conclusive, as regards those geological and historic objections. An examination and comparison of our own with the native antiquarian collections of other European countries confirm the opinion that the gold ornaments discovered in Ireland possess a special character, not found elsewhere.

It has been asserted that the gold of which our Irish ornaments are composed was brought from India by the nomad Kelts who finally settled in Ireland; by some it is supposed that it was procured from Gaul; and by others that it was imported from Spain by the Milesian colonists. Others, again, imagine that it was derived from Africa;—in fact, our manufactured gold has been assigned to every gold-producing country in the world of ancient times, but our own. Again, it has been fancied that these gold ornaments found in Ireland are of Phœnician, Carthaginian, Greek, Hebrew, and even Danish origin; but as none of the asserters of these theories have offered any tangible exposition of them, it is here unnecessary to discuss their merits.

---

* See Rev. Dr. Todd's Presidential Address, in Proceedings for April 14, 1856, vol. vi., p. 326.

www.ingramcontent.com/pod-product-compliance
Lightning Source LLC
Chambersburg PA
CBHW031410160426
43196CB00007B/963